Chronicles of the Damned

Chronicles of the Damned

Malcolm Cheney

Marston House

© Malcolm Cheney 1992

Published in 1992 by Marston House,
Marston Magna, Yeovil, Somerset BA22 8DH
Designed and produced by Alphabet & Image Ltd,
Sherborne, Dorset DT9 3LU

ISBN 0-9517700-3-9

A CIP catalogue record for this book
is available from the British Library.

Typeset by Kendalls, Milborne Port, Dorset.
Printed by Hartnolls Ltd, Bodmin, Cornwall

Contents

Introduction

In the summer of 1978, a friend asked my advice regarding a diary he had found among a batch of household items bought at a house clearance sale. My visitor, knowing that I was a journalist, loaned me the small, thick volume that contained a narrative of events in the death cells at London's infamous Newgate Prison during the years 1823–4. The diary, written in a neat copperplate hand, proved to be the recollections of a philanthropic prison visitor, and his revelations provided a unique glimpse of social conditions and crime in Regency London.

The journal so intrigued me that I decided to elicit as much information about the writer and his stories as I possibly could. So, although a complete amateur in the field of historical research, I nevertheless followed my fascinating quest throughout the ensuing years and came up with much supporting information.

Initially, my friend agreed to my keeping the diary for a while, but eventually he took back his book so that he could sell it. Ironically, he lost it before he could find a buyer. Fortunately, I had managed to photocopy many of its pages and these remain in my files.

The diarist, a Mr Baker, proved an elusive figure to track down. Indeed, I still don't know his first name, where he lived, or his occupation. I suspect that he was one of the more forward-looking of the Church of England's clerics, and probably influenced by the Evangelical Movement. The newspapers of his day have described him as 'a gentleman who generally attends to pray with and give religious advice to the prisoners in Newgate.' The impressions I have formed of him through studying his journal and contemporary press reports are of a humble, kindly man who perhaps had just a little too much faith in human nature, no doubt a weakness exploited by some of the prisoners.

At the same time, he must have had a strong personality, both because of the work he tackled and the success he sometimes seemed to achieve. Even allowing for literary licence in his diary, he does appear to have helped the unfortunate prisoners. He was obviously a person of some importance to the prison; this is clear from the fact that the governor of Newgate was in the habit of calling him in for this unpleasant work, despite the prison already having a perfectly competent chaplain. His philanthropic visits were made on a regular basis over a period of many years.

One example of the consolation that Baker's kind and gentle attentions provided comes in a contemporary press account of the final moments of Anne Norris, a young woman who was condemned for her part in a robbery in the winter of 1821. According to a journalist, Baker helped Norris achieve a mental composure and tranquility shortly before her sad end. So much so, that in response to the chaplain's urging her to 'Be strong in the Lord, and in the power of His might,' she was able to reply with humble confidence: 'I *am* strong in the Lord Jesus Christ.' The writer added: 'Norris was brought out, supported on the right by the Sheriff's Chaplain (the Rev. Mr Dillon), and on the left by Mr Baker. Her fortitude was surprising; and the sight of the congregated multitudes around her agitated her much less than was apprehended. When the cap was drawn over her face, and the rope placed round her neck, and another rope around her clothes just above the knee, she called out. 'Lord receive my spirit,' and then with much emphasis she exclaimed 'Mr Baker, Mr Dillon, God bless you!'

The most important point about Baker's diary is that it is an eye-witness account of actual events, and records conversations that he had soon after they occurred. It provides a rare insight into the minds and feeling of those involved, including Baker himself. It is, indeed, a unique first-hand testimony regarding Regency crime and punishment and their effects on people.

My original research into two of the criminal cases mentioned in Mr Baker's journal resulted in the publication in March 1990 of *A Chronicle of the Damned*, which to my great surprise brought me mail from many parts of the English-speaking world. I was delighted to learn that two of my Australian correspondents were descended from the families of sailor William (John) Castle and Samuel Raines, both mentioned by Baker, and described in my book. Castle's descendant, Mrs Marjorie Carter of New South Wales, has throughout her long life conducted her family history research in the available archives, and she kindly provided me with copies of her material. This has enabled me to prepare a complete picture of the sailor's life right up to his violent death in 1852, and his updated story appears for the first time in print here in this book. In the case of Samuel Raines, it was I who was able to provide useful information to his present-day descendant, Ms Jemma Ussher of Queensland.

Long after Baker had completed his diary, we find his name cropping up in press reports, citing his continued unselfish devotion to the condemned. I fully agree with one of my correspondents who called him an 'angel of mercy', and I feel that his good works should not go unrecorded. I have devoted the chapter called 'Annals of Infamy' to cases described in Baker's diary, and have been able to expand these histories by my own recent researches.

Also of particular interest to my readers, I soon found, were the few incidental criminal case histories I included in my original book. At the suggestion of numerous correspondents I set out on a task which for some curious reason had formerly been sadly neglected: to research and write a varied selection of short histories from the annals of Regency and Victorian crime, which I present here under the chapters headed By the Debtors' Gate and Behind Closed Doors. I have also greatly extended the original notes on the prison hulks and transportation (deportation) system, and have added a brief chapter concerning South London's Horsemonger Lane Gaol.

My thanks are extended to all who have assisted me in this project, particularly to local historian James Wisdom, Michael Armstrong of *Family Tree*, and Tony and Leslie Birks-Hay of Alphabet and Image Ltd.

Malcolm Cheney
London
1992

A slum in London in the nineteenth century.

1 A short life, a long drop

Life in London in the nineteenth century

In 1800 the situation throughout Britain was bad, with many unemployed people, including children, having to exist as best they could at mere subsistence level in slums or even on the streets. And those who could not make it would either turn to crime or end it all by committing suicide.

In London's East End, particularly in the Clerkenwell and Saffron Hill areas, there existed ghettos which were known as 'little Italy' because of the many Italian immigrants living there, and who mostly survived by running small cafes. Those native male Londoners in the same area who were fortunate enough to have work were mainly employed as porters or labourers, whilst their wives and children would earn a pittance in clothing 'sweatshops' or by making artificial flowers. The more enterprising ran market stalls or became shopkeepers in their attempts at upward mobility. With such a large pool of cheap labour available, prosperous families could afford to employ a different servant to perform each individual household task. From time to time, the employed would riot in the streets for higher wages, and naturally the criminal element would join in on these occasions and pick pockets or steal from shops.

For their meals, working men and women would patronise the numerous chop houses – establishments which provided cheap and sometimes wholesome food – and they would also enjoy drinking beer (following the recent tax reductions aimed at discouraging gin-drinking). The chop houses should not be confused with the coffee houses where the better-off gathered to enjoy good company and conversation.

In 1815, when Britain's labour market was flooded by demobbed soldiers at the end of the Napoleonic Wars, it became impossible for

11

most to find work. The only viable alternatives were to emigrate to Australia in the hope of finding a golden future there, to try and make a living by gambling, or to take the more dangerous course of crime, thereby risking either hanging or transportation (deportation) to the colonies.

Prior to the major penal reforms of 1830, one of the thief's problems was finding an offence which did not merit the death penalty: not an easy task because of the difficulty of interpretation of complex laws, depending greatly on the methods of theft, value of the property, and if violence was involved. Death was, in fact, mandatory for the theft of cash or goods above the value of forty shillings, but because the economic climate forced many people to earn a living by crime, both prosecutors and juries often tried to avoid imposition of hanging, mostly by under-valuing the stolen goods. There was also a great deal of leeway in decisions on transportation, much depending on the criminal's record and his reputation.

City crime mostly involved shoplifting, picking pockets, and what we would today term 'mugging', as well as burglary and thefts from ships on the River Thames. Crimes committed in the more rural areas tended towards petty theft and horse and sheep stealing.

Those other victims of circumstance, children, also found it necessary to turn to crime in order to survive on the city streets – for them, it was frequently a matter of steal or starve. Many were orphans, or had been deserted by their parents, but they inevitably shared the common problem of homelessness. Shocking statistics reveal that during the Regency period, the dead bodies of many thousands of children were collected from London's streets, having died from hunger, cold, neglect and disease as well as the criminal actions of others in little better circumstances themselves.

A government report in 1828 declared that:

With the advancement of civilization the darker crimes become less frequent. The whole number of persons tried for offences against the person, in 1827, including robbery of the person, which ought not properly to be included, were under 1,000.

Although the number of offences in the mass of our dense population is very considerable, yet when the subject comes to be examined, security of life and limb was never greater. Property, it is true, is not equally safe; but even here there are not any large

12

proportion of offences which reach to the ruin of persons against whom the offence is committed, or to subject property in general to any very serious risks.

The most usual, numerous and troublesome crimes consist of stealing from the house or the person, goods which are easily transported, and may be quickly converted into money.

This view of the subject is important for two reasons: the one, as it tends to show that with some remarkable exceptions, the state of society is not one of great depravity; the other, that it gives to the operations of government a body which may be acted upon by law. Gangs of pickpockets, pilferers and even housebreakers, may be, to a great degree, controlled and restrained by means of preventive police and exemplary punishment; their crimes are not the impulse of blind passion which is satisfied to sate itself and to suffer for the enjoyment, but the result of a calculation of unprincipled men, on a cool view of their interests. If you can make the hazard greater than the probable gain, you may rest sure you will diminish the crime.

Before the founding of the police force in 1829, offenders were very hard to catch, as law and order were dependent upon an ineffectual system of watchmen, or 'Charleys' as they were popularly known, and a few of what today we would regard as bounty hunters. Crimes would be planned in many of London's 5,000 pubs, and the villains had a ready market for their stolen goods at pawnbrokers' shops, and the many rag and old-iron traders about the city.

Popular opinion regarding crime was often reflected by the behaviour of crowds at executions: the ordinary man in the street would boo offenders whom he or she thought had committed nasty crimes, but would show sympathy for others by remaining silent. The criminal element present on these occasions took the opportunity to pick pockets. However, it seems that all were little moved – and undeterred – by the deaths themselves.

Charles Dickens was present at the execution of the Mannings at Horsemonger Lane Gaol in 1849, and he has left us his impressions of the crowd there on that occasion:

When I came upon the scene at midnight, the shrillness of the cries and howls that were raised from time to time, denoting they came from a concourse of boys and girls already assembled in the

13

The sight of dead bodies dangling from gibbets was an everyday event in Britain's towns and villages during the Regency period.

best places, made my blood run cold. As the night went on, screeching and laughing, and yelling in strong chorus of parodies on negro melodies, with substitutions of 'Mrs Manning' for 'Susannah', and the like, were added to these. When the day dawned, thieves, low prostitutes, ruffians, and vagabonds of every kind, flocked on to the ground, with every variety of offensive and foul behaviour. Fightings, faintings, whistlings, imitations of Punch, brutal jokes, tumultuous demonstrations of indecent delight when swooning women were dragged out of the crowd by the police with their dresses disordered, gave a new zest to the general entertainment. When the sun rose brightly – as it did – it gilded thousands upon thousands of upturned faces, so inexpressibly odious in their brutal mirth or callousness, that a man had cause to feel ashamed of the shape he wore, and to shrink from himself, as fashioned in the image of the devil.

Pathetically inadequate as guardians of the peace, the 'Charleys' patrolled London's streets armed with a lantern, a truncheon, a cutlass and a rattle.

When the two miserable creatures who attracted all this ghastly sight about them were turned quivering into the air, there was no more emotion, no more pity, no more thought that two immortal souls had gone to judgement, no more restraint in any of the previous obscenities, than if the name of Christ had never been heard in this world, and there were no belief among men but that they perished like the beasts.

I have seen, habitually, some of the worst sources of general contamination and corruption in this country, and I think there are not many phases of London life that could surprise me. I am solemnly convinced that nothing that ingenuity could devise to be done in this city, in the same compass of time, could work such ruin as one public execution; and I stand astounded and appalled by the wickedness it exhibits.

As the century progressed and the industrial revolution got under way, and communications and the movement of goods and people about the country vastly improved, more work became available for the masses. Law reforms also gradually eased punishment for crimes, and prison conditions improved with the building of new purpose-built gaols.

But for all classes of folk during this period, the national vice was gambling in all its variations. Rich men preferred to play card games and toss dice in the comfort of their private clubs, and when bored would bet on more eccentric matters. A well-known anecdote worthy of mention here, because of the way it illustrates the total selfishness of these wealthy, bored gamblers, concerns a man who collapsed in a London street – probably the victim of a heart attack. Some gentlemen who were passing immediately laid wagers as to whether the man was alive or dead, and they were furious when sympathetic onlookers tried to revive the victim, because it ruined their bet.

Poor people would try and make easy money gambling on such spectator sports as bare-fist boxing, bear and bull baiting, and cockfighting. This barbarous form of boxing was tolerated for most of the nineteenth century before being banned, whilst bull-baiting, which involved vicious dogs attacking a chained bull, was not prohibited until the 1830s. Charley's Theatre, Westminster, was the favourite venue of those addicted to bear-baiting. But cockfighting was probably the most popular of the cruel sports involving the deaths of animals – a wicked practice which even today still survives in some parts of the world.

This is only the briefest of accounts of the setting in which took place so many of the tragic tales in this book, but fuller accounts of the social ills and penal system of the nineteenth century are plentiful, and easily available. I must now move on to the immediate scene which represented the last resting place of many English felons.

Newgate Prison: 'That School of Vice'

The precise origins of London's infamous Newgate Prison are shrouded in the mists of time, but it certainly served as a City of London and County of Middlesex gaol from as early as the twelfth century. So infamous did it become over the passing years that its very name was synonymous with death, evil, suffering and degradation. Indeed, it thrived in infamy, and was celebrated in fiction, ballad and verse which romanticized the vices and virtues of many who passed through its doors.

After centuries of an enduring misery, a kind of watershed was reached in 1780 with the attempted destruction of the prison during the Gordon Riots. But the gaol survived and was promptly rebuilt, to remain on its site near Smithfield Market until 1902. It was an imposing edifice, as befit its purpose, being a large, solid, grim, rusticated building located on the corner of the Old Bailey and Newgate Street. Besides having cells and yards it contained a chapel, and was surmounted by the Keeper's lodgings.

The prison housed over 400 half-starved inmates of both sexes, adults and children. And they existed in appalling conditions: the rations were meagre, and no beds, uniforms, combs or towels were provided. Soap was a luxury. Most inmates had to sleep on the floor on verminous rugs and mats, as only a privileged few were allowed to have their own beds moved into the prison. Bribery and gambling flourished, with currency being clothing, food, tobacco and newspapers.

The male side of Newgate comprised an unholy mix of those awaiting trial, some serving sentences for minor crimes, capital convicts awaiting either death or transportation to the colonies, and the boy prisoners. From the early 1800s, the women had a marginally better deal, segregated as they were into the tried and untried. The children and some of the more privileged women were allowed to attend a special prison school.

The improvement of the women's lot followed the establishment by the Quakers in 1817 of the Ladies' Prison Visiting Association headed by the indomitable and legendary penal reformer, Mrs Elizabeth Fry. To the amazement of many, this admirable organization soon diverted many of the women prisoner from their 'idle, abandoned, riotous and drunken ways'. This remarkable transformation was apparently achieved by the provision of carefully supervised paid work and education, and by the governesses setting the unfortunate women personal examples in 'industrious and orderly living'.

But there were no such rehabilitation opportunities for the men. They were further educated in only one subject at Newgate – the profession of crime! This was emphasized in an 1827 government report: 'It must be confessed,' it admitted, 'that of late years the art of crime, if it may be so called, has increased faster than the art of detection. The improvement of communication, the employment of young thieves by the elder and more practised, the crowded state of our gaols, and other causes, have tended in many parts of the country to make the plunderers of property a species of organized society, having their division of labour, their regular leaders, and premeditated means of escape.'

Newgate's Ordinary (prison chaplain), during our diarist Baker's time, was the Rev. Horatio Salisbury Cotton, supported by his deputy the Rev. Springett. By the standards of his day he had a humane, enlightened approach which did much to ease the sufferings of the convicts. A measure of Cotton's concern can be judged by the fact that he established a school for children at the prison within six weeks of his appointment in 1814. Mrs Elizabeth Fry said of him: 'He has been very kind to us, and I think has been very attentive to the prisoners; very frequent in visiting them in all cases of emergency, especially when they have been under sentence of death and near execution.' And she described his friend Mr Baker as being a white-haired old man who had for years 'devoted much time and attention to unostentatious but invaluable visits in Newgate.'

In common with British prison conditions today, Newgate was grossly overcrowded in 1818. Almost half its population of 460 were under the age of 20, many of them boys and girls in the 9–16 years age group. Cotton was anxious to reform them and keep them away from the bad influence of adult hardened criminals. But his efforts at educating and clothing them were met with both ingratitude and abuse, as was clearly revealed at a government inquiry in 1818. Cotton reported that leather and a shoemaker were provided for the school in an early attempt to teach the lads a trade, but the boys stole the good leather which they exchanged for bad leather they had smuggled in. And when some shoes were finally made and paid for, the youngsters damaged them out of sheer malice. So the scheme was abandoned.

Outside the debtor's door of Newgate Prison scaffolds were erected overnight for public executions the next day.

Other wretches who were practically naked on their admission to Newgate were provided with footwear and clothing, most of which they soon sold. Cotton added that boy prisoners also sometimes stole from visitors, one even going so far as to steal a handkerchief from a visitor's neck.

Despite his efforts to reform and care for the children, Cotton had no illusions about them, and reluctantly had to accept that the religious instruction he gave them had little or no effect, as they generally returned to crime immediately they were released from prison. The job of teaching them to read and write was left to the schoolmaster, a former slave trader who was serving a seven year sentence. The only children banned from attending the school were those under sentence of death.

As well as caring for the prisoners' material and spiritual welfare, Cotton showed a great concern for the sick and the condemned. At that time, those awaiting death were usually kept three to a cell, a practice which Cotton greatly deplored. He told the government committee he thought the condemned should be kept in solitary confinement, believing this would have a beneficial spiritual effect, and this was instituted soon after. He thought that isolation would avoid 'scenes of indecent mirth occasioned by the profligacy of one or two, when the others were decorous or penitent.' He also disliked the practice of convicts being put into irons on admission to Newgate, and felt that if they were not ironed they would be more amenable to moral instruction.

Executions were customarily held at Newgate on Monday mornings, and the condemned sermons were preached on the preceding Sundays. Cotton approved of some members of the public being admitted to the prison chapel to hear the condemned sermons, feeling them advantageous to the public and the cause of morals, and that 'the execution is intended as an admonition to people not to fall into those courses.'

Attendance at the gloomy prison chapel was compulsory for the condemned and those recently reprieved from death sentences. The Ordinary usually asked some other prisoners also to be present, generally women and children, as well as some of the more penitent of the men. The chapel could accommodate some 350 people, and the visiting public often occupied about half the space on these dreary occasions.

The condemned prisoners were forced to sit around a coffin in the notorious 'black pew' in the prison chapel to hear a sermon on the day before they were to be executed.

When Dr Cotton took over in 1814, he tried to end the degrading and distressing custom of featuring a coffin in the proceedings. The coffin had taken pride of place, mounted on a table in full view of the offenders, throughout the service. But to Cotton's dismay, the practice was nevertheless revived from time to time at the insistence of the Gaol Committee of Aldermen.

By 1828, the public was excluded from the prison chapel on the days that the condemned sermons were preached. But, as Mr E. Gibbon Wakefield revealed in his publication on the subject that year, the Sheriff and his deputy attended in state, wearing their gold chains, while behind their pew stood a couple of tall footmen in state liveries. Wakefield adds: 'The Sheriffs were in one gallery; in the other opposite were the convicts capitally convicted who had been respited. Down below between the galleries was the mass of the prison population; the schoolmaster and the juvenile prisoners being seated round the communion table, opposite the pulpit. In the centre of the chapel was the condemned pew, a large dock-like erection painted black. Those who sat in it were visible to the whole congregation, and still more to the Ordinary, whose desk and pulpit were just in front of the condemned pew, and within a couple of yards of it. The occupants of this terrible black pew were the last always to enter the chapel.'

A graphic account of proceedings during a condemned sermon appeared in a June 1825 issue of *The Times*, and it makes interesting reading, conveying vividly the atmosphere of the sad and solemn occasion. Among those mentioned in the press report are William Probert, aged 33, condemned for his complicity in murder; 30-year-old horse thieves William Sergeant and James Harper, and burglars John Smith, 28, James Goff 21, Edward David Dunn and Edward Crawley both 17.

The death sentence on Probert so affected his mind that his dark hair was reported to have turned grey in just a few hours. And right up to the time of his execution he both hoped and believed that he would be reprieved. But it was not to be. The only one who was spared was Edward Crawley, who turned informer shortly before he was due to die. Here is part of the newspaper story:

At half-past 10 o'clock, the prisoners confined in Newgate were conducted by the various officers to the chapel. Of those who are to die, Probert entered first. His appearance was just such as might have been expected by those who read the accounts in general circulation about him. He walked with a firm step to the pew appropriated for those who are irrevocably doomed to death. He sat down, put his hands to his face, and seemed to be quite overpowered with anguish. He neither looked up nor down, nor did he pay the slightest attention to the words addressed to him by Mr Baker, who has been unremitting in his religious labours on the occasion. Next to him sat Smith, who presented a strong contrast to his neighbour, and fervently prayed during the service. Sergeant and Harper, who are also to die, were farther off; and beyond them sat Goff, Dunn and Crawley, who are to die this day week...

Probert seemed to disregard all that was passing before him, until the Ordinary came to that part of the Litany which refers to wife and children. He then moaned, and some thought he shed tears.

The Ordinary expatiated generally upon the effect of repentance, exhorted those to whom he particularly addressed himself, to place their whole reliance upon Christ, and called upon God to supply them with the spirit of cheerful resignation and fortitude in the moment of their last trial. There was not ... a single allusion in the address to the case of Probert. It had mere reference to the general guilt of the condemned, and it gave not the shadow of hope to any of those who have been ordered for execution. The other culprits it exhorted to penitence, which still might have the effect of making them recognized and useful members of society. Probert revolted at the sound of the words 'to die'.

As soon as the Ordinary concluded, Smith, who sat next to Probert, stood up, and in a most earnest tone, called upon those around him to look upon what was about to take place next day, as an example of what must inevitably occur to them, if they persevered in the course of profligacy which had brought them to their present condition. He called upon the three unfortunate persons who are to suffer death this day week, to prepare for the change, and upon those who are about to die with him, to pray to God for patience.

Upon hearing this address, several of the female prisoners screamed aloud. Some of the condemned men were also affected. The chapel was soon cleared of its wretched inmates, and Probert and the rest of those who are to suffer, were conducted back to their solitary cells.

The plan of informing the condemned of their fate was, we understand, different upon this occasion from that usually adopted. All those [34 in number] who were included in the report were gathered together in the condemned room, for the purpose of hearing the result. The effect of thus congregating the prisoners was dreadfully impressive, and not one felt the bitterness of disappointed hope so keenly as the most desperate among them [Probert]. His limbs shook, and when he could distinctly speak, he said, ' Oh God, is this the way, am I to die? Oh, it is not for this I die?' All attempts to recover him from his fears and his horrors were useless. His whole soul was fixed upon life, and between the hope and the fear he has remained ever since.

The site of executions was transferred from Tyburn to the outside

23

Officials chat in the Press Yard at Newgate while the prisoner's irons are removed, before his hands are tied and he is led out to the gallows.

of Newgate Prison in the winter of 1783, and some of the more sordid accompaniments were abandoned, but the public infliction of death still remained. This was a situation that was to last for a further 85 years, until public hangings were finally ended in 1868. And during that period many and varied were the crimes of the felons who ended their lives outside the debtors' door at the prison.

What was claimed to be an innovative ingenious invention was featured outside Newgate Prison in the winter of 1783. Called the 'new drop' – a portable gallows with a collapsible platform – it replaced the outdated and inefficient old cart method, and the first culprits to benefit from this new technology died on 9 December that year. (In earlier days, it had also occasionally been the custom to hang people near the scenes of their crimes, but this occurred only three times after 1783.)

For some years the Newgate gallows were kept very busy. In 1786 there were some 96 executions, but as the years passed and laws and public opinion changed, the number of hangings gradually decreased.

The new gallows in the Old Bailey were first used in 1783. Eighteen out of every twenty hanged were under 21, and some were children as young as 9.

As early as 1809, the former Surgeons Hall across the way from Newgate Prison in the Old Bailey had been demolished and replaced by a new Sessions House where capital crimes were tried. A subterranean passage, covered with a metal grating which dimmed the light of day, linked both buildings for the convenient and safe transfer of prisoners. It was along this dismal passage, about half an hour before scheduled executions, that officials including sheriffs, prison governor and surgeon, would proceed to the gaol from the courthouse. The solemn parade would wend its way to an open courtyard within the prison where it would join the waiting captives and accompany them to the Press Room for pinioning.

This done, and after a short wait for the prison bell to begin its doomful tolling, the governor would give the signal, and the condemned would be escorted to the scaffold, led by the Ordinary reciting from the burial service as he went.

What happened next is best described by an eyewitness:

At the little porch leading to the gallows the sheriffs and officers stop. But the clergyman ascends the steps with the prisoner. The chaplain takes his place on the little line of sawdust which marks the outline of the drop which falls, and which without such a signal to denote its situation might easily be overlooked in the dusky black of the well-worn apparatus. The prisoner, with arms closely pinioned behind him, then takes his place beneath the beam. Following close is the common hangman, who at once pulls a white cap over the condemned person's head and fastens his feet with a strap. The hangman then shuffles off, usually amid hisses from the crowd.

After the drop fell, the executioner or his assistant would often, out of sight of the public, swing on the legs of the poor unfortunates who had not died immediately. This was to break their necks and thus put an end to their sufferings. The bodies were customarily left to hang for an hour before being cut down and then sold by the executioner to grieving relatives or friends for burial. But if the criminals had been condemned to dissection, then their corpses were withheld, put in sacks and taken away to hospital by cart.

Some unscrupulous hangmen would often make quick cash by the distasteful practice of selling pieces of the fatal ropes as well as the deceased's clothing. And some executioners even decapitated the bodies to enable death masks to be made for sale to the public.

A contemporary account of the death of gentleman-forger Henry Fauntleroy provides us with another vivid description of a Newgate execution in 1824.

Fauntleroy, a 41-year-old unmarried London banker, was convicted of swindling clients by the use of forged documents. Inquiries revealed other thefts totalling the then staggering sum of £170,000. Rumours ran rife throughout the city that Fauntleroy had spent the cash on gambling, drink and women ... allegations he strongly denied, saying he used the proceeds of his crimes on building speculations to bolster his failing business. But it proved a hanging matter, and he died before a crowd of an estimated 100,000 people. Here is part of the London journalist's report:

At midnight the carpenters began to erect the scaffold, and from that time it may be said the crowd, which was anxious to witness the execution, commenced to assemble. As the morning advanced, the crowd proportionally increased, and about six o'clock a continued line of persons might be seen hurrying through Fleet

Street, Holborn, Cheapside, and other principal streets which lead to the Old Bailey.

At eight o'clock the crowd was immense. Not only did the multitude extend in one compact mass from Ludgate Hill to nearly the beginning of Smithfield, but Skinner Street, Newgate Street, Ludgate Hill ... places from which it was impossible to catch a glimpse of the scaffold ... were blocked by persons who were prevented by the dense crowd before them from advancing further. Every window or house roof which could command a view of the dreadful ceremony was likewise occupied. Within the railing, in the area immediately surrounding the fatal platform, were placed, in a double row, between 300 and 400 constables.

Fauntleroy was described as a stout man of middle height, with grey hair and a pale complexion. He was short-sighted and wore glasses. His manners were 'easy and gentlemanlike, and bespoke his having being accustomed to genteel society.' For his execution he wore a black coat, waistcoat and trousers, with silk stockings and shoes. After his arms were pinioned inside the gaol, Fauntleroy was led out to the gallows escorted by officials and clergy, including our diarist Mr Baker. The writer continues:

As the mournful procession passed down stairs and through the gloomy passages leading to the place of execution, the Ordinary read, as is customary, part of the burial service, and the bell of the prison clock tolled the death-knell. The prisoner never turned his head to the right nor the left till he reached the foot of the steps leading to the scaffold. The moment he appeared on the scaffold the vast crowd took off their hats, and the noise and confusion which had heretofore prevailed was succeeded by breathless silence and 'attention still as night'. We could not at this moment see Mr Fauntleroy's face, but we understand that he did not open his eyes even for a moment. Mr Springett and Mr Baker, who had accompanied him to the foot of the scaffold, pressed his hands and left him. They seemed much affected.

The executioner without a moment's delay, pulled the cap over the prisoner's face, and over that tied his neckcloth across his eyes, which we believe is not usually done. The rope was likewise adjusted with equal expedition; so that in less than two minutes after the unhappy criminal ascended the scaffold, everything was prepared for his execution. Mr Cotton now placed himself before the prisoner, who stood with his face towards Ludgate Hill, and commenced to read a passage from the bible; towards the conclusion of which the trap-door fell. No expression of feeling proceeded from the crowd. The poor criminal did not appear to suffer much; just a few convulsive heavings of the shoulders were observable, but they ceased in a few moments.

In about a quarter of an hour, the crowd began to disperse; but many remained to witness the cutting down of the body, which took place a few minutes after nine o'clock. Workmen immediately set about removing the scaffold, and in a short time nothing remained to denote the dreadful scene which had passed.

Hepworth Dixon, author of *The London Prisons*, published in 1850, noted the moral evils of public executions, and was particularly perturbed by all the sordid related activities and public disorder which attracted the very worst elements of society, at what was claimed to be a religious ceremony gravely enacted for the good of society:

> This is, in truth, our circus ... our gladiatorial arena. We Christians, who talk of Rome with measureless pity and contempt ... as a nation of angels might do ... here prepare our feasts of blood. We do not fill our theatre with wild and famished animals, to gloat over them while they tear each other to pieces; but we only give another direction to the cannibal instincts of our people, and gratify them after a fashion peculiarly our own. The scenes enacted in front of Newgate disgrace us in the eyes of Christendom.
>
> And the example ... is it effective in deterring others? We fear not.

With admirable foresight, he concludes: 'If death punishments be continued ... and we are convinced that they need be continued only provisionally ... they should be secret, but at the same time swift and certain; surrounded by all the terrors of an unseen by inexorable doom.'

In fact, executions were carried out within the prison from 1868, with only officials and representatives of the press as witnesses. A black flag was then hoisted to announce to the public that hangings had taken place. The condemned were buried within the prison, and their clothes were burnt.

After a long and colourful history, Newgate Prison was finally demolished in 1904, and the present Central Criminal Courts building, more popularly known as the Old Bailey, was erected on the site.

The final photograph of Newgate Prison before demolition.

'Whatever little remains of innocence or honesty a man might have is sure to be lost there.' Convicts regarded prison hulks like the 'York', illustrated above, as a hell on earth, worse than Newgate.

2 Prison Hulks and transportation

Apart from hanging, Britain's transportation (deportation) policy proved an easy option for ridding the country of many of its convicted criminals, as well as saving the expense of building and staffing prisons to hold them. At the conclusion of their sentences, it also provided reformed convicts with a new chance in life with the many job opportunities then available in the pleasant climates of Australia and Tasmania.

A spell aboard a hulk (prison ship) was the usual prelude to transportation aboard a regular ship to the colonies, and during their wait for a voyage convicts were employed at hard labour in the dock yards; in some cases they even replaced horses to haul timber.

The hulks

In 1828 there were ten hulks, containing some 3,900 prisoners, located at various places around the country, including Sheerness, Woolwich, Portsmouth, Chatham and Gosport. The hulk *Euryalus*, a former Royal Navy frigate stationed at Chatham, was a vessel holding about 300 boy offenders aged between 8 and 16 years. The conditions aboard the hulks were appalling, the food practically inedible, and sanitary provision almost non-existent. Punishments included whipping, close confinement and deprivation of food. But a government Select Committee report of the same year decided that:

Transportation for life is an excellent punishment in certain cases. Where a man has made crime his habit and profession; where he has become the chief or a member of a band of thieves, and has no resource on his return from imprisonment but to herd with the same gang and pursue the same practices, it is both mercy and justice to spare his life, and remove him to a distant colony, where he

31

may first afford an example of punishment by hard labour, and by degrees lose his vicious propensities in a new state of society.

Transportation for fourteen years is far from having the same advantages with transportation for life. For those who dread the loss of their native country, it gives a hope of return, which greatly diminishes the value of the punishment. The returned transport, likewise, is generally a very abandoned character, and he usually returns to his old criminal society, thus forging a link, as it were, between the thieves at large and the thieves under punishment.

The committee also noted that transportation for seven years was at that time seldom resorted to, but usually commuted in practice to confinement for four or three years on board the hulks.

Prison Discipline Society Chairman, Samuel Hoare, said he thought prisoners discharged from the hulks were manifestly hardened in depravity. And he added: 'A man may get over being in gaol, but the hulks is quite fatal. It is a stigma upon a man.' Asked about the state of the convicts aboard the hulks which he had recently visited at Portsmouth, Hoare observed that, 'there being confined together so many must have a very contaminating effect.' He continued: 'and their labour by day ... having seen them employed at different times ... is merely an apology for work; one sees them idling about the yard, several of them together drawing a light cart, which perhaps a donkey might draw quite well.' But Hoare considered the association of convicts at night one of the most insuperable evils in the hulks system. On this very point, a committee reported that:

Neither the Captain, nor any other officer, ever visits the parts of the ship [hulk] in which the prisoners are confined, after the hatches are locked down, except upon some extraordinary emergency, or in cases of disturbances, which very rarely occur. And it seems doubtful whether, in some of the hulks at least, an officer could go down among the prisoners at night without the risk of personal injury. The guards never go among them at night. Under these circumstances there can be no doubt of the prevalence among the convicts of gambling, swearing, and every kind of vicious conversation.

It appears, that from the time which convicts are locked down within their several decks in the evening, until the hatches are opened in the morning ... a period which in the winter includes nearly two-thirds of the 24 hours ... they are left entirely to themselves, without any of the officers or guards to inspect them, and without any other control over their conduct, than the knowledge that any riotous noise or disturbance will be communicated by the guards, who are on watch in other parts of the vessel, to the officers, and will be followed by their interference.

One or two of the convicts themselves are selected by the Captains of the hulks to act on each deck as boatswain's mates, whose duty it is to take care of the lights kept burning on the deck, and to call out to the watch from time to time to inform him that 'All is well'; and if the guard has any observation to make upon what is going on below, he addresses himself to these persons, but they exercise no authority over the other convicts, nor would they venture to mention openly to the Captain any irregularity or offence of which their fellow-prisoners should be guilty. The Captains state themselves to be in the habit of communicating privately with many of the convicts, from whom they obtain intelligence concerning the character and behaviour of the rest, but it seems admitted, that the individuals from whom such information is derived cannot be brought forward to prove the facts, from the danger to which they would in that case be exposed of being ill-treated by their companions ...

Upon on the subject of the manner in which the convicts employ themselves at night, that if any noise like rapping or hammering is heard after a certain hour, they are desired to go to bed, it being known that they are making money, hammering out crowns and half-crowns into sixpences.

A typical daily routine aboard a hulk in 1828 has been described as follows:

At gun-fire ... a quarter before six a.m. ... all hands are called. At six o'clock, prisoners lash up their hammocks, and there being then but one watch on duty, an additional one is called previous to the release from their cells of such prisoners as do duty aboard; at a quarter past six, breakfast is served down under the inspection of the officer of the morning watch. The hours for sending prisoners on shore to labour depend on the time when dockyard workmen resume their employment; they are mustered out of the ship in

33

gangs, and received on shore by the officers, quarter-masters and guards; the latter strictly searching their persons to prevent the concealment of anything tending to facilitate an escape, or contrary to the rules and orders of the ship.

At half past seven a.m. those prisoners appointed to do ship's duty proceed, under the direction of an officer, to clean the ship fore and aft, which is ready for inspection by half past nine; a part of the officer's duty also is to muster and lock into a cell appropriated to that cause, prisoners complaining unwell, where they are visited by the surgeon and his assistant; and should the cases require it, admitted into hospital. This measure of confining them prevents their straying into other parts of the ship, or committing, should any feel so disposed, depredations on the properties of their fellow prisoners.

On the return of prisoners from labour, which commences about a quarter before twelve a.m. the same precautionary measures of searching their persons previous to entering the ship ... to prevent their bringing on board any property belonging to the dockyard ... are resorted to, and the whole are generally on board and mustered into their respective cells by a quarter past twelve, when two watches are set, each consisting of an officer, quarter-master and five guards, the greater part of which, with the two officers, are stationed between decks. At half past twelve dinner is served down; at a quarter before one the aforesaid watches are relieved by two, who remain on duty until half past one, when the prisoners are again ordered up, and after going through the same examination of irons and persons as in the morning, they proceed to labour about a quarter before two.

When all hands are on board, such new prisoners as may have been received within the last month are called, and made to pass athwart the quarter-deck in presence of the officers and guards, with their hats off, whereby their features, walk and person become familiar, in case of attempting disguise to effect escape. This portion of duty ended, an officer is stationed at the hatchway forward, to overlook the quarter-masters, who muster down the whole, each man carrying his hammock. Two officers, with a guard in each deck, receive them below, and see that every prisoner retires in an orderly manner to his cell. At a quarter past six supper is served down; and a quarter before seven ... Saturday evenings excepted ... the prisoners who attend school are summoned from their respective divisions into the chapel by the officer on watch, where they are received by a quarter-master and guard. At a quarter before eight o'clock, an officer and his watch being stationed in the body of the chapel, the remainder of the prisoners are collected to hear evening prayers read; which ended, the whole are mustered and locked up in their respective cells for the night.

The Occurrence Book contains a detailed account of the proceedings of each day, commencing with the total numbers victualled, distinguishing those on hospital diet, the number on shore, and on ship's duty; the names of the officers and prisoners, termed Inspectors, who attended the receipt of issue of provisions; the attendance of the chaplain and surgeon; the absence of officers or guards, and from what cause arising; the receipt, death or discharge of the prisoners, their offences and punishments; the number of prisoners at school; and, in short, any incidental transactions that may occur; the whole concluding with the names of several officers who attend the evening prayers. An abstract of such weekly proceedings is sent to the superintendent in London every Sunday. Attached to this book is kept a small one, wherein, for a more distinct view, the offences and punishments of prisoners are registered. The Character Book, containing every prisoner's name and age, form a register of their conduct each past quarter, under the different denominations of very good, good, indifferent, suspicious, bad, and very bad.

It is the duty of officers to enforce good order, cleanliness, and a strict adherence to the rules of the ship; to issue new and cause the old clothing to be repaired; to keep a slop book as a check on the great one in the office; and, at the end of each quarter, make a return to the Captain of the quantity of slop [clothing] received from the stewards, and issued by them to the prisoners under their care.

The rules seemed quite humane and reasonable, but the reality was a different matter. An eyewitness view of life aboard the hulks was graphically recorded by an educated criminal called James Hardy Vaux, a confidence trickster who served no less than three terms of transportation. Writing about a hulk at Woolwich, he said:

Of all the shocking scenes I have ever beheld, this was the most distressing. There were confined in this floating dungeon nearly 600 men, most of them double-ironed; and the reader may conceive of the horrible effects arising from the continual rattling of chains, the filth and vermin naturally produced by such a crew of miserable inhabitants, the oaths and execrations constantly heard among them. Nothing short of a descent into the infernal regions can be at all worthy of comparison with it. All former friendships or connection are here dissolved, and a man will rob his best benefactor or even messmate, of an article worth one halfpenny. The guards were commonly of the lowest class of human beings; wretches devoid of all feelings; ignorant in the extreme, brutal by nature, and rendered more tyrannical and cruel by consciousness of the power they possess. No others but such as I described would hold the situation. They invariably carry ponderous sticks with which, without the smallest provocation they will fell an unfortunate convict to the ground, and frequently repeat their blows long after the poor sufferer is insensible.

Vaux explained that the new prisoners were allotted to the lowest of the ship's three decks where bilge water plagued the occupants. It was, he said, up to the individual prisoner then to either bribe or fight his way through the upper decks to gain a marginally better existence.

Vaux claimed the guards took great pleasure in flogging convicts at the slightest excuse, and then rubbing salt into their wounds. Other punishments included heavy weights being attached to the irons which they already wore day and night, and solitary confinement in the ship's dreaded 'Black Hole' which was often deep in bilge water.

The food, also, was appalling. One prisoner complained: 'You can just break the bread in two and throw a bit against the wall and it will stick like clay.' Vaux said that the water in which the beef was boiled was thickened with barley, and formed a mess called 'smiggins'. He added that the cheese was mostly bad, and that the beef consisted of old bulls, or cows, which had died of age or famine.

It was impossible to enjoy any semblance of personal hygiene on the hulks as there was minimal sanitation, no regular change of linen, nor were combs and towels provided. And the prisoners' clothing and bedding were infested with vermin.

Although some convicts had cheated the gallows in exchange for transportation, many died of disease that often swept through the prison hulks. In July 1832, Hulks Superintendent John Capper described an outbreak of cholera among convicts at Woolwich and Chatham. He said: 'During the last four months the cholera has prevailed to a very great extent, and although attended with much loss of life, the proportion of deaths compared with the number of cases has been far less than average in society at large who have been attacked with that disorder.' He claimed that the lower fatalities were due to the dedicated attention of his medical officers. But less than a year later, in February 1833, Capper reported a further outbreak causing numerous deaths. Other diseases which periodically decimated the prisoners included consumption, dysentery, smallpox and scrofula.

An unexpected and sometimes fatal danger that always faced the hulks was mud, and in 1829 an incident cost the lives of three convicts. Some time prior to the event, Captain George Loyd, owner of the *Dolphin* hulk moored in the River Thames, had sensed that all was not well with his high-sided, somewhat top-heavy vessel which was supported by piles. He had even confided his fears to Hulks Superintendent John Capper, and the ship's hammock house was subsequently removed to ease her. Three days before the accident, several tons of mud which had gathered around the hulk were removed by lightermen using a steam engine. But on the fatal midnight soon after, the ship was still gripped fast by mud as the tide came in, and the vessel would not float. Instead, it fell over on one side as water flooded in through the scupper holes. Three convicts were trapped inside and were drowned. An eyewitness recalled later:

As the convicts were making violent efforts to escape, Capt. Loyd unfastened six of the wards [cells]; the other two were forced open by the prisoners themselves, who rushed in a body to the hatchway. The others got out of portholes, the iron fastenings of which were with difficulty broken. Upwards of 100 of them escaped. They got ashore with no other clothing than their shifts, when they were guarded by the military, and some of them remained in that state for nearly four hours. While the *Dolphin* was stuck fast in the mud, the shaking caused by the endeavours of the convicts to escape made her spring out of the mud, and she heaved over to the opposite side; she tottered for a few minutes and then fell over on her side.

The coroner's jury was of the unanimous opinion that the *Dolphin* was improperly constructed for use as a convict ship, and recommended that another vessel, or some other means, be adopted to prevent similar accidents.

When convicts in Newgate found out through the grapevine that they were about to be transferred to the hulks, they rioted and caused as much damage as possible. Questioned on the matter by a government committee in 1818, Newgate Keeper William Brown said such prisoners caused much destruction. He described how the convicts were removed from Newgate 25 at a time in an open, chest-high caravan drawn by six horses with a mounted military escort. They were not ironed in the caravan, except for a light chain from their legs, and although they could not escape their arms were free. The prisoners were frequently unruly during their long journey to the hulks and, when passing through towns en route, tried to break windows by throwing whatever they could lay their hands on.

Some convicts, who Brown thought 'decent, respectable and well-behaved', were occasionally allowed the privilege of travelling with him in his chaise, while others were grouped together in the caravan to separate them from the worst villains. In bad weather, Brown gave the prisoners suitable clothing, as well as the regulation rations for the journey. For the longer journeys, each man was allowed a loaf of bread, tea for their breakfast, three quarters of a pound of beef, and two pints of beer.

But sentencing men to transportation and actually getting them from the prisons to the hulks were entirely different matters, and convicts often tried to escape en route, sometimes successfully. In November 1829, twelve prisoners made an escape bid while travelling by coach from Chester to Chatham. The journey had all the elements of a rattling action-packed yarn that would have done justice to a historical novel.

The convicts were escorted by three guards: Chester Castle gaol's head turnkey George Hillige, guard James Davies, and a gardener called John Roberts. Just why Roberts should have become involved in the affair is not clear, but he took on the escort assignment at the suggestion of a local magistrate. The party boarded the Albion coach at 8 a.m. and was soon heading for Birmingham. All went well until they reached Walsall, when the horses suddenly got out of control. The coachman tried to rein in the animals but, together with Hillige and Davies, was tossed off the speeding coach. When it was finally halted, the convicts were locked in a nearby building while Roberts looked for his colleagues. He found Davies badly bruised and shaken, but Hillige had two broken legs.

After a two-hour delay, the coach got under way again, arriving at the Albion Inn, Birmingham, at about 9 p.m., where the prisoners and their two remaining guards (Hillige was left behind at Walsall) transferred to another coach for Coventry.

Roberts rode inside the coach with three of the convicts. They sat opposite him, each fastened to a chain by a handcuff on the left hand and with a shackle on each leg also fastened to a chain. The other prisoners and Davies were on top of the coach.

A brief stop was made at Coventry for a change of coachman, and the journey was resumed, only to be halted again for a few moments while Roberts and Davies changed places. Davies needed the comfort of the inside of the coach because he was in pain after his fall. As they switched over, Davies warned Roberts to be very vigilant. One can only guess at the thoughts that may have passed through Roberts's mind as he sat on top of the coach as it sped along the dark, rough road, its lamps casting dim pools of light through the lonely countryside on that chilly, winter night. He could not be blamed for perhaps thinking that the drama of the trip had already been played out, but any such thoughts were to be short-lived.

Roberts, who was unarmed, sat at the rear of the coach with five convicts, two beside him and three opposite, all of whom were secured to his chain. Another four offenders sat on the roof near the front, just behind the coachman and guard on the box.

It was shortly after 1 a.m. when the convicts made their move. Four of them suddenly pounced on Roberts and dragged him off his seat at the same instant as the coach lurched into the side of the road and stopped, leaning to one side. The convicts forced his hands behind his back, and one of them, later described by Roberts as 'a lusty man with grey hairs in his head, wearing a round sailor's jacket and dark trousers,' tied his hands with a cord while others searched his pockets for the handcuff key.

Roberts pleaded with the prisoners to free him, but one replied: 'We cannot loose you. We want our liberty, and our liberty we will have or lose our lives.'

Whilst the convicts undid their handcuffs, Roberts was aware of a commotion from inside the coach. He later learned this was a fight between Davies and prisoners, which ended with Davies being badly beaten and left inside the coach with his hands handcuffed behind his back.

All the convicts then got off the coach and started to knock off their leg irons with a chisel and the metal slipper of the coach, but they were interrupted after about ten minutes by seeing a light approaching in the distance. They immediately split into groups and hobbled off across the fields. One man had already freed himself from his leg irons and run off.

The light proved to be the lamps of the Alliance coach from Liverpool, and shortly before it arrived at the scene the Albion's coach guard freed himself and released Roberts from his bonds. Roberts shouted out 'Murder!' to warn the people in the Alliance, but it contained only an elderly gentleman who was unable to help.

Both coaches then travelled to nearby Dunchurch, but Davies and Roberts could not get help there because of the absence of the principal constable. The pair then hitched a ride aboard the Alliance back to Coventry, where police formed a search party of ten watchmen and others. Meanwhile, Davies and Roberts obtained a stagecoach and four horses, and all the searchers returned to the scene of the escape. Dawn was breaking as they arrived, and they split into groups to scour the countryside.

Seven convicts were eventually recaptured, but the remaining five had disappeared, never to be recaptured.

At sea

The main hazard for transportees, of course, was to survive the four months journey to the other side of the world in overcrowded and insanitary ships, and the dangers of shipwreck. By the early 1800s ships' captains and surgeons were encouraged by the promise of cash rewards to care for their convicts: the healthier the prisoners were on arrival in Australia, and the lower the journeys' death roll, then the higher were the rewards paid to the officers.

It is not surprising then that the male transportees created relatively few problems for their captors during these long voyages. But the behaviour of many of the women prisoners, who travelled in separate ships, often proved troublesome.

It took a military force to put down a disturbance of 194 female convicts at Cork Gaol, where they were confined in the winter of 1827 before being shipped to Australia aboard the *Elizabeth*. Several soldiers were hospitalized during the riot of what a Board of Inquiry later called 'the worst and most turbulent female convicts ever embarked at Cork.' And their behaviour did not improve during the non-stop trip to New South Wales, where they arrived in March 1828.

The Rev. John Vincent, an Anglican clergyman on his way with his family and servants to work in Australia, dared to express his 'disgust and abhorrence of the womens' licentious behaviour'. He complained that many of them spent the night with seamen and indulged in drunkenness, riot, fighting and debauchery. Vincent said: 'The very air resounded with their curses, imprecations and obscene language,' which he claimed was tolerated by both the ship's master and the Surgeon Superintendent Joseph Hughes, who was in charge of them.

Poor Vincent would have been well-advised to have remained silent on the matter, for it brought down on his head both the anger of the prisoners and resentment of the crew. Describing his plight in a letter to the Inspector General for New South Wales, Dr Edward Trevor, the clergyman said almost all his boxes and cases were broken open and his property either damaged or stolen by women and the crew, who had access at all hours to the forehold where the belongings were stowed. He explained: 'Part of my rations had been refused me at the beginning of the voyage, viz. tea, sugar, wine, lime juice, etc., and I must add to this that hampers of wine and porter, and two kegs of spirits were very considerably plundered before I had the possibility of knowing it. Almost all my poultry were taken, one sheep was killed, and a milch goat on which my infant, then in a most delicate state of health, chiefly depended for her sustenance, was poisoned. This rendered our situation absolutely miserable, and what increased our sufferings was that we put into no port during the voyage. We arrived at Sydney in truly pitiable and emaciated condition.'

At the end of the voyage, Vincent complained to the authorities, and a Board of Inquiry upheld his grievance. After a searching investigation, the Board found that the prisoners had not always been mustered into the prison each evening at sunset (a convict even fell overboard and drowned late at night); that locks of the prison were often picked at night; and illicit intercourse had taken place between women and some of the crew.

But the board admitted that Surgeon Hughes was very deaf and many irregularities could easily have been committed without his knowledge. Hughes, a middle-aged medical man who had served in the Royal Navy with distinction for more than twenty years, and had been a prisoner of the French for several years following his capture during a naval engagement, strenuously denied the allegations. His fate, however, and that of the ship's master, Walter Cock, rested with Britain's Home Secretary Sir Robert Peel, who expressed his 'very strong dissatisfaction' at their conduct, and both were expelled from the service in disgrace. They were also deprived of the usual cash reward for good conduct at the end of the voyage.

The inquiry seems to have led to no improvements in the long run, however, for some years later in 1833, two seamen, John Owen and John Richard Price, complained of the behaviour of some of the 108 female convicts aboard their ship the *Amphitrite*, which was wrecked in a gale off Boulogne while en route to Australia. This was reported in *The Times*, October 1833.

Owen and Price, two of the only three survivors of the wreck, said later that the language and behaviour of some of the women had been 'outrageous and disgusting' beyond anything they had ever seen. Owen, the ship's boatswain, claimed he had frequently had to throw pails of water over women as the only means of keeping them away from the crew. Owen, a survivor of thirteen shipwrecks, told a journalist he believed it a general rule on board female convict ships to keep the prisoners away from the crew. But in this case, because of the indifference shown by Surgeon Superintendent Forester, who was in charge of them, the convicts went practically anywhere they liked so long as they did not create a disturbance.

The only punishment given was for riotous behaviour, when the offender was placed in a wooden sentry-type box on deck where she was left for hours at a time. Because of the lack of room, the sufferer could not sit down in the box, which had no opening except for some small holes at the top to admit air. There was no reward or encouragement for good conduct, and no attempt was made to keep the women employed. And the Captain never interfered with them in any way, as he felt it was not his business to do so.

Owen said divine service was not held on board, but that each woman had a bible given to her by penal reformer Mrs Elizabeth Fry and two other Quaker ladies prior to the voyage. He noted that he had seen very little kindness among the prisoners, but that they had not generally seemed to be dejected, nor regarded transportation as a punishment. Indeed, many of them had said they meant never to return to England.

From time to time, letters would appear in the columns of *The Times* deploring the bad state in which convict ships were allowed to go to sea, and the frequency of transport shipwrecks during the early years of the last century more than justified the concern. The vessels were privately owned and hired out to the government for the long and dangerous journeys to Australia.

Only two years after the sinking of the *Amphitrite*, yet another female transport, the *Neva*, went to the bottom near King's Island, Australia. Only 15 people, 6 prisoners and 9 crew, of 241 survived the tragedy. And in August 1842, two British ships were wrecked together off Table Bay. The vessels on that occasion were the troopship *Abercrombie Robinson* and the *Waterloo* convict transport. Although the soldiers were landed in safety, 183 convicts perished. After a careful examination of every part of the wreck of the *Waterloo*, a Board of Enquiry found that the vessel had been unseaworthy. Captain J. Marshall, who headed the inquiry, declared that, 'The general decay and rottenness of the timbers appeared at every step we took. Insufficiency of either iron or copper fastening was manifest in some of the timbers and planks of the original construction, many of which appeared crumbling to dust with age and rottenness.' A writer for *The Times* took up the criticism:

Having before us the report sent by the board of officers to the admiral on that station, we feel that no personal considerations ought to restrain us from expressing a feeling of regret that there should have existed such good reasons for censure.

This report states, that during the gale the master was on shore, that the *Waterloo* was left under the charge of an inexperienced

*Afull and Horrifying Account
of a most dreadful*

SHIPWRECK

**Of the Neva, Convict Ship,
Which sailed from Cork, for
New South Wales, in May
last, containing 241 Souls on
Board, consisting of 150 female Convicts, 9 free Women,
and 55 Children, all of whom
perished except 6; and 9 of
the Crew; with an Account
of the dreadful Sufferings of
those who were saved, while
staying on a desert Island,
being altogether one of the
most heart-rending Accounts
of Human Suffering which
has occurred for a very long
Period.**

young man; that she had no third cable on board; that the masts were not cut away to lighten the ship; that the longboat was not got out; that the quarter-boats were equally neglected; in a word, that no measures were taken to avoid the worst and most probable consequence of the gale.

Dreadful as were the actual consequences of this inefficiency and unseamanlike mismanagement, they fell far short of the horrors which only a providential interference averted from the unhappy convicts.

The prisoners had been ordered below, from a fear that they would crowd into the lifeboats that might have come off to their rescue: they were then bolted down; the corporal of the guard affixed a padlock to the bolt, and locked it without orders. In the general panic he forgot to unlock the door; and, had not one of the prisoners been provided with a hammer, all the wretched crew would have been consigned at once to a helpless and disregarded doom.

An unnamed ship's Surgeon-Superintendent, who safely supervised some 600 convicts during four voyages to Australia in the 1820s, has left us a somewhat rose-tinted description of what life was like aboard a convict transport.

Before leaving the hulk, the convicts are thoroughly clothed in new suits and ironed [put into irons]; and it is curious to observe with what nonchalance some of these fellows will turn the jingling of their chains into music whereto they dance and sing. Two rows of sleeping berths, one above the other, extended on each side of the between-decks of the convict ship, each berth being six feet square, and calculated to hold four convicts, every one thus possessing 18 inches space to sleep in ... and ample space too!

Scuttle-holes to open and shut for the admission of air are cut out along the ship's sides; a large stove and funnel placed between decks for warmth and ventilation; swing stoves and charcoal put on board, to carry about into the damp corners; and in fact everything that can be thought of provided to secure health and proper comfort to the convicts during their voyage.

The prisoners were, in fact, confined to the tiny berth space for 20

45

Men were penned like cattle below decks of convict ships en route to Australia.

out of every 24 hours, being allowed to exercise only two hours each morning and two hours in the afternoons.

The surgeon added that bibles, testaments, prayer books and psalters were distributed among the convicts, and he claimed that the rations 'were both good and abundant', comprising a daily allowance of three-quarters of a pound of biscuit, with a dinner of either beef, pork or plum pudding. And to prevent the men from succumbing to scurvy, each was given an ounce of lime juice and sugar every day. The sick, he observed, were given medicines and made comfortable.

He concluded: 'The common diet of the convicts is certainly more than is requisite to keep them in health, as they have no work to do; but it is not more than is politic to allow them, because if you stint them on the voyage you must keep them under greater restraint, and their healths will suffer in consequence.'

Life in Australia

The ending of the Napoleonic wars in 1815 resulted in a crime wave in Britain, partly due, no doubt, to the lack of employment for the demobilized soldiers. At the same time, there were claims that transportation was no longer an effective punishment, and rumours abounded that transported convicts were prospering because of the fortunes which could easily be made in Australia. So many optimistic opportunists either committed crimes in order to be transported, or went to New South Wales as settlers.

A transported convict's fate on reaching Australia or Van Diemen's Land (Tasmania) was rather a matter of pot luck. The government's policy was that on their arrival '... they shall be subjected to different degrees of severity according to the magnitude of their crimes, and the notoriety of their former course of life. Criminals of the most hardened character will be subjected to confinement in the most penal settlements; and those whose crimes have been less enormous and of whose reformation some hopes may be entertained, will be subjected to severe labour on the roads and in chain gangs. The minor class of offenders will be distributed as servants assigned to work for their masters, subject in all respects to the control and authority of the Governor.'

Convicts were classified by age and trade, and allocated work accordingly, the more skilled men usually being assigned to government projects. Most were destined for private employment, and this was particularly beneficial for the government because the convicts had to be housed, clothed and fed by their civilian masters.

In 1819 the British Government sent J. T. Bigge to review the Australian colony. His recommendations were that, wherever possible, convicts should be removed from the temptations of the city of Sydney by reducing the number employed in government public works there, and that instead most should be assigned to private service in the outback. Bigge thought that re-offenders should be sent to specially harsh penal settlements, which he said should be expanded, for severe punishment. Subsequently, between 1820 and 1840, the regulations were tightened up and convicts were generally treated more severely than before. In 1823, Governor Brisbane introduced 'clearing gangs' to work on the roads, clearing land for government farms and on that allocated to settlers. These convict labourers were usually chosen from those who had displeased their civilian masters, or as a disciplinary punishment.

Those who were lucky enough to be placed with good civilian masters, and who served their time well without misbehaving or trying to escape, could expect a decent future in their new country. This was confirmed by reformed transportee Jorgen Jorgensen, who in 1834 wrote: 'This is the common effect of transportation on all prisoners in Van Diemen's Land. The new scenes and occupations in which they are abruptly placed, like the transplanting of a tree, make them suffer for a time, until restraint becomes a habit, and, in both body and mind, the convict becomes a new man.'

The amount of clothing and rations issued to convicts in service were ordained by the government, and statistics for 1838 reveal that this weekly entitlement was as follows: 7 lb of mutton or beef, or 4$\frac{1}{2}$ lb of salt pork, 12 lb of wheat, and two ounces each of salt and soap. A yearly issue was made of two jackets, two pairs of trousers, three shirts, a hat or cap, and three pairs of shoes. Some of the more considerate masters also gave their convicts extra tobacco, tea and sugar, as a reward for good behaviour.

For women convicts, the situation was rather different. Those who were not kept in prison usually became domestic servants or factory workers, or were even granted tickets-of-leave if their husbands were in the colony. And although those who were kept under lock and key did not generally try to escape, unlike their male counterparts, they could nevertheless be a nuisance as they often rioted, and some of them succeeded in seducing their guards. But by law they were not allowed to be flogged, neither were they ever to be sent to the penal settlements.

In 1835, a special institution for juvenile offenders was opened at Point Puer. This was a centre for 'hardened' lads aged between 8 and 18 years, where they were taught a trade, as well as learning to read and write, with the aim of placing them as apprentices with the colony's tradesmen. Commenting on this establishment in 1852, the Rev. John West wrote: 'It is refreshing to find that kindness and coercion were united in the discipline of Point Puer: an oasis in the desert of penal government. When the boys were submissive and diligent, they were not forbidden to be happy: they trained as tailors, shoemakers, carpenters, boat builders, masons and gardeners. Some became acceptable apprentices and are now respectable men.'

A magistrate had the power to sentence prisoners to flogging or death. Here the official remarks, 'I will give the damned wretch a hundred lashes and send him to be hanged,' and the hangman by the gallows replies, 'It's complete butchery but I must do it, I suppose.'

Flogging was the most common form of convict punishment, although it was forbidden that they be whipped by their civilian masters, and magistrates toured the colony to judge allegations of mis-behaviour and prescribe sentences. Statistics show that in 1833 in New South Wales, 9,000 lashes were ordered in just one month, and that in neighbouring Tasmania, over the same period, 4,250 lashes were carried out among the 15,000 convicts there. Other summary punishments included solitary confinement and the treadmill. Harsher still was a period of hard labour on the roads, with or without irons. And there remained, of course, the ultimate retributive deterrent – banishment to a penal settlement.

The road parties and iron gangs were generally under the over all command of a military officer, with deputies in the form of convicts used as overseers. Soldiers guarded the prisoners around the clock, and stern discipline was administered. The famous Quaker, James Backhouse, who visited the colony in 1836, complained that the soldiers often used provocative language, mixed with curses, in speaking to the convicts. 'This,' he observed, 'is of bad influence in hardening them, when they greatly need to be rendered more susceptible of good.' The unfortunate men worked 14 hours each day in tropical temperatures, and at night were confined in 'Belly Bots', portable huts on wheels holding up to 30 men who had no room to lie down.

Commenting on their harsh treatment, Backhouse explained: 'Here, the punishment to which they are subjected for misconduct in the gang is flagellation; and in some instances they have received from 600 to 800 lashes within the space of 18 months, at the rate of not more than 50 lashes for one offence.'

However, it was claimed that 'a fate worse than death' awaited those who were destined to serve time in any of the colony's penal settlements. The most notorious of these outposts of hell were located at Moreton Bay and Port Macquarie in New South Wales; and at Port Arthur, Macquarie Island and Maria Island in Tasmania. And, of course, the dreaded Norfolk Island off the continent's eastern coast.

Commenting on these awful places, Chief Justice Forbes said: 'The experience furnished by these penal settlements has proved that transportation is capable of being carried to an extent of suffering such as to render death desirable, and to induce many prisoners to seek it under its most appalling aspects.'

Tasmania became a separate colony in 1825 under the command of a Lieutenant Governor, and a new penal settlement was set up at Port Arthur on the Tasmanian Peninsula in 1830. It was thought that dangerous prisoners could be more efficiently and economically controlled there, and be sent out to the various constructional works on the island as labour gangs.

Were it not for a narrow strip of land named Eaglehawk Neck, the Tasman Peninsula would be an island, and it was this fact that made the place ideally suited as a penal outpost. To escape from Port Arthur, it would have been necessary to cross the narrow isthmus, difficult enough with normal guarding arrangements, but virtually impossible when the unique new guard system was introduced. From shore to shore across the centre of the Neck, a line of vicious dogs was tethered on short chains, so that there was only a short space between each. The line was continually patrolled by soldiers and constables, with watching posts on the hills, and so effective was this system that very few prisoners ever pierced the line. A further deterrent was that it was rumoured that the surrounding sea was infested with sharks.

A large town eventually grew out of the business of imprisoning convicts – some 12,500 served their sentences in Port Arthur – and the ruins of the major buildings are still to be seen today. The settlement operated until 1877, when it was abandoned and the convicts transferred to the then new Hobart Gaol.

Although today's official tourist literature plays down the horrendous side of prison conditions, stating that convicts were held in clean, well ventilated buildings, and were better fed than the soldiers who guarded them, a sorry tale of unmitigated misery has come through other sources. The only inhabitants of this dreary gaol were the prisoners and their keepers; the work was both exhausting and hazardous, and the punishment was terrible.

Absconding was considered the most serious offence a prisoner could commit, and it drew the severest penalties. 'Habitual absconders,' as even today's official government literature admits, 'would gradually lose all freedom, progressing from 50 lashes through confinement on bread and water, the chain gang in irons, to the final degradation of the bucks stalls ... separate compartments on a public road where they were chained to a wall and employed at breaking stones.' Other incorrigible prisoners were punished by assignment to the nearby mines which were feared and described by all as being a 'hell on earth'. Some cells were built in the mine galleries, and failure to complete allotted tasks resulted in floggings or solitary confinement underground.

A unique invention may be credited to the engineers who designed the convict-operated tramway built between Long Bay and Norfolk Bay. It was Australia's first railway, and the half-ton carriages were propelled by four convicts who pushed up the hills and rode downhill. Runners were changed halfway to operate this system of transporting passengers and supplies over a seven-mile route.

Prison conditions were no easier at the other penal establishments, especially at Norfolk Island, of which its chaplain, the Rev. Styles, observed sadly: 'Blasphemy, mutual hatred, and the unrestricted indulgence of unnatural lust are the things with which a short resi-

Convicts in Port Arthur who were punished a second time had to propel officials in an iron carriage on a seven-mile railway.

dence in the prison wards must necessarily familiarise the convict.'

Because of the harsh conditions and the lack of hope, escape became the order of the day for most convicts. And despite the fact that the penal outposts were located in isolated spots, convicts frequently did escape their captors, but the odds against them successfully fleeing the colony were against them from the very start. The nature of the country, with its harsh environment, was the main obstacle, as well as the lack of food. Also, the natives would often kill escaped convicts or deliver them up to the authorities for the reward. Some escapees would team up with bushrangers, many of whom were men who had deserted their civilian masters and formed gangs. They lived either by highway robbery or by raiding the homes of settlers. Their careers usually ended either in death in shoot-outs with the military, or by hanging following their recapture.

The more ambitious would try and get out of the colony. In 1825, one gang successfully hi-jacked the ship *Eclipse*, sailed off and were never heard of again. Two years later, other convicts seized the schooner *Phoebe* and went to Tahiti, only to be recaptured and returned to Australia for punishment. In January 1834, a gang of eleven comandeered the brig *Frederick* and sailed to distant Chile. But fate caught up with them in the form of *HMS Blonde*. Although seven convicts escaped, four of their less fortunate comrades were returned to Tasmania and duly hanged.

Yet other escapees would stow away on vessels in the harbours, and put themselves at the mercy of ships' captains once well out at sea. Some of these men were allowed to work their passages to distant ports where they were freed. But most were returned to their prisons and brutally punished.

A notorious and horrific case of escape, murder and cannibalism, which occurred in 1823, has since become part of Tasmania's folklore, and is told with the sort of dramatic detail that follows. It involved Irishman Alexander Pierce, who at the age of 26 was transported for seven years for stealing six pairs of shoes. Initially, his tale was no different to that of dozens of other convicts who followed a continual cycle of escape, capture and punishment. But Pierce was a stubborn man, and he was determined to gain permanent freedom, no matter what the cost.

After several escapes and recapture, Pierce one day fled from the Macquarie Harbour penal institution together with seven other prisoners – Badman, Brown, Cornelius, Dalton, Greenhill, Matthews and Traverse. They remained together for ten days, during which time they had no food except for their kangaroo-skin jackets which they ate, being nearly exhausted with hunger and fatigue. On the eleventh night, they consulted on what was best to be done for their preservation, and decided upon ... cannibalism!

Not surprisingly, next morning three of the convicts had disappeared, and were thought to have returned to give themselves up. But the five remaining escapees then drew lots as to who should die. It fell to Badman's lot, and he was killed while Pierce and another went off to collect dry wood and make a fire. When they returned, they found Traverse stripping the body of flesh which they used as food for a few days.

The next to die was Matthews. When he had been eaten, Traverse could not continue the journey through fatigue and lameness in his knees, so Pierce killed him on the spot. The two survivors, Greenhill and Pierce, then made their way as best they could, carrying Traverse's flesh between them, in the hope of reaching the eastern settlements while it lasted. But by the time the food was almost gone, the journey was far from completed. And it seemed to Pierce that Greenhill, who always carried the axe, was seeking an opportunity to kill him. Neither man now dared sleep. The fire lived, died and was replenished as the night wore on, and still both men refused to submit to sleep. But finally, the warmth from the blaze eased Greenhill into a fitful slumber. Pierce made his move: on hands and knees he slowly approached the circle of light that ringed the fire and illuminated the dozing convict. He crept nearer and reached out for the handle of the axe which had slipped from the grasp of Greenhill's fingers. Pierce, axe in hand, silently rose to his feet, and grasping the weapon in both hands raised it high above his head, casting a sinister shadow in the flickering firelight ...

Replete after his meal, Pierce continued his journey alone. Walking due east, he soon left the protection of the forest to cross a wide, grassy plain. After many days without food, living only on grass and nettle-tops which he boiled in a tin pot he carried with him, he at last reached some natives' huts, which from their appearance had only just been vacated. He searched around for food and quickly made himself a meal from kangaroo entrails and scraps of meat. After resting a while, he again staggered off across the plain.

Although near collapse from hunger and exhaustion, Pierce's luck held. Two days later he came upon a hut in the High Plains, some 70 miles distant from the prison, amply stocked with food. He rested up there for a fortnight before finally deciding to travel to the nearby River Clyde and surrender to a magistrate.

But fate again intervened on his behalf, for on his way to give himself up, he met and teamed up with two bushrangers. After only a few weeks of freedom, however, the trio were captured by soldiers and hauled off to Hobart Town gaol. Pierce's companions were speedily tried and executed for their capital crimes, and he himself was returned to the Macquarie Harbour penal settlement, as an absconder.

Despite the fact that he went about his labours heavily-ironed as part of his punishment for escaping, Alexander Pierce was soon planning a further bid for freedom, and this time he decided to take only one other convict along with him, a man named Thomas Cox, who was equally keen to flee the inhuman conditions he was enduring.

Their chance came on a wet November day when they were among a party of convicts chosen to work in the woods near the prison. Each armed with an axe, they found it simple to lose themselves in the undergrowth, where Cox struck off Pierce's irons before they made off into the wet thicket. Progress was slow and tempers flared from time to time, particularly at night when they could not succeed in making a fire no matter how hard they tried. For several days they travelled on in this way, without food except for shrubs and shoots from the tops of trees, before on a Sunday evening reaching Pierce's first objective, the King River.

For many miles in either direction the river flowed through a deep gorge surrounded by densely-wooded hills, and Pierce aimed to cross the river, scale the tree-clad heights and head north-east, following the coast to Port Dalrymple. But he was furious to discover a totally unexpected problem – Cox could not swim! And if they were to remain free it was essential that they crossed the wide river.

Fuming, Pierce helped Cox make a fire while they discussed how to make the crossing. But their talk led to sharp words, and then to blows. Pierce hit Cox three times on the head with his axe. Thinking him dead, Pierce prepared to leave but was surprised to hear Cox plead in a faint voice: 'For mercy's sake, come back and put me out of my misery!' He obliged by striking Cox a fourth time, this time making quite sure that his victim was dead. Then followed the by now ritual routine of stripping the corpse of its more edible flesh and roasting some of it for supper.

Next morning, Pierce swam across the river with the intention of going on to Port Dalrymple. But then a strange thing happened, his conscience at last caught up with him. As he was to put it later in his own words: 'My heart failed me, and I resolved to return and give myself up.'

Stricken with remorse he recrossed the river, and threw away the flesh he was carrying for food. Some time later, he saw the schooner *Waterloo* under weigh for the settlement, and he made a signal fire on the beach. William Evans, coxwain of the *Waterloo*, put off in the pilot boat and was met by Pierce, whom he already knew. He fastened Pierce's hands, and a search of the prisoner's clothing revealed a single piece of flesh. Asked what it was, Pierce said: 'It's a piece of Cox, and I brought it to shew that he is lost.'

Later, back at the penal settlement, Pierce admitted to the Commandant that he had murdered Cox. Asked why he had killed him, he answered: 'I'll tell no man, until I am going to suffer.'

The next day, Evans returned to the scene of the crime with Pierce, who was to help him recover what was left of the body. Evans was horror stricken at the scene: the head and hands had been cut off the body, the bowels torn out, and the greater part of the breech and thighs gone, also the calves of the legs and fleshy parts of the arms.

'How could you have done such a deed as this?' asked Evans.

Pierce replied: 'No person can tell what he will do when driven by hunger.'

A few yards away under the shade of a tree, Evans found the head and liver of the deceased, and an axe stained with blood. The fragments of the body were naked, and near them were some pieces of shirt and the cover of a hat. There had been a fire near the body, and not far from it lay a knife. The hands were never found.

After a full confession of the happenings of both escape attempts, Pierce was eventually tried, convicted and hanged. As a final irony, the judge ordered that his body be delivered over to the surgeons for dissection.

Other, less gory, accounts of escape from the penal colonies are well documented, among them the tragic tale of George Robinson. In 1843, he appeared in the dock at Liverpool Assizes charged with having illegally returned from transportation, and a crowded court listened attentively to Robinson's account of his misadventures.

His troubles started in 1820, when at the age of 18 he was convicted of highway robbery at Pendleton. Initially sentenced to death, he was reprieved and transported for life. But Robinson soon experienced 'an irresistible desire' to return home, and not long after his arrival at Sydney he made an escape bid by swimming to a brig lying offshore and hid aboard until the ship was at sea. But the vessel had to return to port because of bad weather, and Robinson was sent to the penal settlement at Hunter's River where he received 100 lashes.

He was later transferred to the penal outpost at Macquarie Harbour and put in irons for a year. In this awful situation, shut off from the world and his friends, he determined to escape again. He eventually did so with several others, but the party of runaways was attacked by natives three days later. Several convicts were wounded in the encounter, and the natives stole all their clothes and provisions. The escapees nevertheless pressed on and soon lost themselves in the Blue Mountains where they roamed naked for two months, living on what they could find. On reaching the cost near Port Philip, they were captured by more natives and handed over to the authorities.

Still naked, they were taken to Coal River where they were given a single blanket to cover them, but they had to leave it behind when they were put aboard a government boat which was shipping coal to

Sydney. Had it not been for a piece of canvas, the prisoners would have had to lie naked on the coals in the hold. A public charity supplied the men with clothes on their arrival in Sydney. Their punishment was 100 lashes each and further incarceration at Macquarie Harbour.

Still determined to escape, Robinson soon absconded again with others, and they sailed off in a whale boat which followed the coast for nine days, with the aid of a makeshift sail made by tying the men's shirts together. But, because they ran out of food, they put into Hobart Town, were re-arrested and sent back to Macquarie Harbour. This time, however, they were put on Big Island − the depot for incorrigible prisoners.

Robinson said the horrors of the place were 'more than language can paint'. He added that several prisoners committed murders so that they might be sent back to Sydney for trial, although they knew they faced certain death for their crimes.

Robinson remained at Big Island for seven years before being returned to Hobart Town. Undeterred by his bitter experiences, the convict again escaped, hid aboard ship, and handed himself over to the captain after three weeks at sea. The captain, however, gave him up on arrival at St Helena. A seven-months spell as a prisoner on Robins Island followed, where he was hampered with 25 lb of irons upon him. Again, he was returned to Macquarie Harbour, but during the voyage he showed remarkable bravery during a gale, and he was recommended for mercy. Finally, after three more years, he was released into the colony on a ticket-of-leave.

Despite all his misfortunes he still suffered homesickness, and he escaped aboard an American whaler in which he cruised for several months. But on learning that the captain intended to surrender him at the first opportunity, he sought refuge with some friendly natives on reaching New Zealand. Robinson had some good luck soon after, and without suspicion he took passage to Boston. From there he travelled to Greenock and then on to Liverpool. For some time he lived in Manchester where he made an honest living.

It was not revealed how he was apprehended. But he told the court that he hoped his sufferings and subsequent good conduct would earn him mercy. The magistrate said that Robinson's tale would help dissipate the idea that transportation was a light punishment. However, he said that it was his duty simply to pass on Robinson the sentence that he should be transported again for the term of his natural life. The prisoner bowed respectfully and was removed from the bar.

A journalist felt that Robinson's appearance was 'calculated to procure credence for the history he related'. And the writer added: 'There was a remarkable expression of suffering and hardship in his countenance, and there was something very moving in the manner in which he received the sentence that was to consign him again to the horrors he had been describing.'

Transportation was finally abolished in 1853, following the pressure of a long campaign by Australia's anti-transportation movement, formed in 1847.

3 Annals of infamy

One particular story from the diary of Mr Baker starts on the evening of Friday, 19 March 1824, when he is called to Newgate by the prison governor, who asks him to accompany him while he announces reprieves to some of the prisoners but confirms the death sentence on others. He writes:

> The governor communicated to the convicts the results which in general was most favourable, only three out of the number were ordered for execution, two on the Tuesday following, viz Samuel Raines and J. A. Wren for maliciously assaulting J. Collins with a pistol with intent to rob him ... and at Execution Dock on 2nd April, William (John) Castle, a sailor convicted at the Admiralty Sessions for stabbing his Captain with intent to kill.
>
> Many who received mercy were overwhelmed with gratitude and fell on their knees to return thanks to God who had delivered them from such imminent danger.
>
> Castle and Wren seemed to receive the awful news with assumed courage and indifference. Castle said: 'Well, I can die but once. I can't help it.' Wren immediately took up a tobacco pipe, and charging it began to smoke with an apparent carelessness. Raines seemed much agitated and distressed in his feelings.

Castle's case

John Castle was a young sailor who had suffered the barbarous punishment sometimes handed out to erring mariners in those violent times. My own research revealed that although born into a poor family, Castle had a better start in life than did many of his contemporaries in an age of widespread poverty. His parents managed to place him with the Marine Society's training ship *Solebay*, anchored at Greenwich, and he went on to become a merchant seaman.

The declared aims of the Marine Society were: 'To receive poor distressed boys, and send them out into sea service. They are provided for on board a ship until they can be placed out in the King's service, or the East India Company's service, or in the merchant service.' The Society was not subsidised by the government, but run by a committee of 'about sixty merchants, naval gentlemen, East India directors, and some elder brethren of the Trinity'. The government's sole contribution to this worthy cause was the provision of the ship, which had already seen better days. The organisation had an office in London where financially distressed parents throughout the country could apply to have their sons admitted to the training ship which had a superintendent, schoolmaster, cook, boatswain, two mates and a carpenter. If lucky, their children would be among the 400 boys accepted each year. Age was not important, but the lads had to be healthy and a minimum of 4 feet 9 inches tall. They were provided with free food, clothing and education. If they proved suitable, then after about eight months they would be chosen for sea service by the owners and captains of ships who visited the *Solebay* from time to time for that purpose. Boys were rarely kept on by the Society for more than a year.

Castle made his first voyage, to Malta and back, aboard the *Weymouth* store ship, returning home in 1812. Then followed a brief but colourful naval career in the best Errol Flynn movie tradition. According to Baker, Castle, who was later described as being 5 foot 5³/₄ inches tall, with grey eyes, brown hair and a fresh complexion, led a life of 'unbounded sin, depravity and debauchery' between voyages to St Helena, East Indies, Australia and India.

Castle told Baker that his troubles really began in 1823 when he deserted his ship at Bombay during a return trip from Australia. He claimed that Captain John Welham Clarke, master of the *King George IV* freetrader, later enlisted him at Bombay as a foremast man, knowing he was a deserter. He said they had agreed on the pay he was to earn plus a cash advance, but the Captain went back on his word and refused to pay him until he could find a bondsman; so Castle walked off the ship.

At Castle's London trial for attempted murder, Captain Clarke said he was arrested, returned to the ship and was not punished, but confined to irons for refusing duty. Castle claims that he was flogged, put in irons, but at length permitted to go to his work, but not

60

in this situation he continued about
5 Weeks when some fresh altercation
took place owing to his treatment,
upon which the Captain insisted
on having him flogged a second time
This so irritated him, particularly
as it was a holiday, being Easter
Sunday, that he ran at his perse-
-cutor as he thought him, with a
knife he had in his hand, scarce
knowing what he was about & struck
at the Captains head — He was im-
-mediately taken by the mate &
his Shirt stripped off, tied up & they
were ordered to flog him, but the rest
of the Sailors refused to obey, the
mate then ordered a Rope to be rove
to hang him up immediately, but
some Military officers who were on
board as passengers, interfered and

A page from Mr Baker's diary.

allowed his full proportion of support like the other sailors. Baker continues:

> In this situation he continued about five weeks, when some fresh altercation took place owing to his treatment, upon which the Captain insisted on having him flogged a second time. This so irritated him, particularly as it was a holiday, being Easter Sunday, that he ran at his persecutor (as he thought him) with a knife he had in his hand, scarce knowing what he was about and struck at the Captain's head. He was immediately taken by the Mate and his shirt stripped off, tied up and ordered flogged, but the rest of the sailors refused to obey. The Mate then ordered a rope to be brought to hang him up immediately, but some military officers who were on board as passengers, interfered and prevented it.

The 'fresh altercation' turned out to be an accusation of theft against Castle by a fellow-seaman, an allegation he hotly denied, but the Captain nevertheless ordered him to be punished before the crew. Captain Clarke said at Castle's trial that, 'Whilst the men were coming aft to witness the punishment, I continued walking up and down on the quarter deck. Castle was on the same side and was not then tied up. I stopped against the capstan to give an order, and Castle was then close behind me standing still. I felt a sudden blow on my face and I heard a voice say, 'You b . . . . . . I'll be hung for murder.' I knew it was Castle's voice, and I knew there was no-one else nearer to me in that direction than the helmsman. I put my hand to where the blow was given, and I stumbled and fell and felt blood running down my face. The surgeon was called, and I was confined a week or ten days.'

Had he known what torture was to come, Castle might well have wished he had been summarily hanged. Baker's story continues:

> He was again put in irons, hands and feet, fastened to the deck without any shirt to screen the heat of the sun which rose blisters on his back, and remained in that situation till they arrived at the Cape of Good Hope, after traversing 300 leagues in that distressing condition. He was taken very ill from his exposure to the weather day and night, during which time he had nothing but bare planks to lie upon. He was removed apparently lifeless and placed under the doctor's care by whose humane attention by

using proper means for his recovery, placing hot water to his feet and stomach he was restored. But shortly after ordered on deck again and placed in the same situation, but still the doctor shewed him great kindness, although the Captain severely reprimanded him for it.

From that time, he was kept in irons as described, till his arrival in England, being 102 days; and two hours each day throughout the voyage, his handcuffs were unscrewed to fasten his hands behind him in order to make his punishment more severe.

Once back in England, Castle was speedily tried at the Admiralty Sessions and convicted of attempted murder. He was then committed to Newgate where he shared a death cell with Raines and Wren.

The day after announcing their execution dates, Mr Baker returned to their cell early in the morning. His journal continues:

I resumed my visit, endeavouring to draw their attention to the short period of time which then remained in their right use and improvement thereof; whilst thus setting before them the solemn prospect of eternity which they were very shortly to enter, and its dreadful consequences to the finally impenitent.

Castle burst into a flood of tears, sighing most deeply, and said 'Oh Lord, have mercy upon me. Oh, what a great sinner I have been.' Wren seemed to catch the same spirit, and confessed himself most guilty also. I felt most happy in observing this change of feeling, and on my retiring was pressed most earnestly to visit them again as soon as possible.

At the close of the day I again visited the cells, and on retiring left the three young men in a composed and resigned frame of mind.

It was a peace of mind that was to be short-lived, as is graphically described by Baker when he tells of Raines and Wren being taken away for execution:

This was indeed a trying moment, and there was no acting in it, but all was most sincere; distressed and afflicted nature expressed its overwhelming feelings in its truest sense. It was a tragic scene that drew tears from the gaoler's eye and must have softened the most obdurate heart.

Castle seemed petrified, and a sudden horror appeared in his countenance and deathlike paleness o'er spread his cheek.

He gazed at each one around, and with the greatest anxiety said to me: 'Oh, sir. What are they going to do?'

I said: 'The time is now arrived to separate, bid them a final adieu, and retire. Pour our your feelings to God in secret prayer in their behalf.'

He burst into a flood of tears again; he embraced his fellow-sufferers and retired, while I walked forward supporting Raines, who again and again most earnestly pressed me to see his wife and endeavour to console her. 'Oh,' he said 'how awful. Oh, what a shameful end am I coming to. Lord have mercy upon me.'

Castle having retired, immediately fell on his knees, weeping aloud and praying most fervently for the poor departing creatures. Such indeed was the exemplary conduct of this young man that it was observed by the bystanders. It was difficult which to admire most, his manly fortitude, his sympathetic tenderness or his fervent piety.

After the executions, Mr Baker tried to console Castle:

Castle now became the chief object of my attention. While I visited him morning and evening of each day I found him gradually advancing in faith and hope, till at length, his consolations seemed to abound. On one of my visits, he was dwelling much on the comparative happiness of his mind when contrasted with his former state. He said he found himself an entirely new creature.

I answered this must be the case if he expected happiness hereafter. 'For if any be in Jesus Christ, he must be a new creature. Old things must pass away, and all things become new.' This was a spiritual declaration. 'But,' said I, 'let us try and search diligently into the true state of your mind in this respect. Now considering your former pursuits; suppose you could be delivered from your present trials, and could be surrounded by your jovial companions inviting you to a cheerful dance, to drink deep in the intoxicating cup, or mix with the loose, abandoned and profane, and join in their noisy mirth and revelry which afforded you the greatest pleasure and delight ... could you, do you think, resist such inviting and alluring scenes as these?'

'Oh, sir,' said he, 'I know what these allurements are full well; but believe me, they never afforded me any pleasure like that I have lately experienced within these cells while meditating on the mercy of my saviour in affording me the means of deliverance from my sins and revealing to my heart a sense of his pardoning love ... no pleasure is to be compared with this, and I really think I could find no happiness in my former pursuits. Nay, when I think on them, my mind is truly distressed on account of them, for they have indeed been most sinful, and could my life be spared, I think I could not possibly return to such folly and such sin.'

From his line of questioning, it is possible that Baker already knew through the grapevine that Castle would not hang. The authorities in London granted him a reprieve and sent him off on another voyage; but this time he did not work as a sailor in the foremast rigging. Instead, after a brief spell aboard the *York* prison hulk, he was shackled below decks on the ship *Mangles* en route for a lifetime exile in Australia. The ship sailed from Portsmouth on a warm July day. Castle was just 24 years old.

However, Castle, who was apparently a plausible rogue, had well and truly pulled the wool over everyone's eyes, as my further research in the Tasmanian archives showed. While convincing Baker that he was a repentant and changed man, Castle conveniently failed to mention that he was already an escaped convict on the run from Australia. He had escaped a year earlier while serving 14 years transportation imposed by a Woolwich Court Martial. Our diarist, had he known it, would have been very disillusioned by Castle's subsequent career.

On arrival in Sydney, Castle was assigned to serve the Rev. Samuel Marsden, who in turn ministered to two flocks – a human one, and a more profitable one in the form of his 1200 sheep. As well as being a farmer, Marsden was also a magistrate and was feared for his severity. No wonder then, that in March 1828, Castle was being tried at Sydney General Sessions as a notorious runaway and kept aboard the *Phoenix* hulk before being finally shipped out to the penal settlement at Moreton Bay, New South Wales. Castle had, in fact, been caught in the most unfortunate circumstances. He was spotted purely by chance working as Mate aboard the colonial schooner *Alligator,* under the assumed name of John Smith. His discoverer, Dr Nesbitt, a convict ship Surgeon Superintendent who remembered Castle from a previous voyage, immediately reported his suspicions to the authorities. Castle was arrested, his true identity established, and was sentenced to serve three years in the penal settlement. Had he been allowed to remain free and keep his job, then perhaps Castle might thereafter have led a blameless and happy life.

Castle may well have reflected on the irony of this situation during the ensuing years in a long and painful prison existence which ended with his execution for murder in 1852. And probably, while in the death cell at Hobart Town gaol in Tasmania, he vividly recalled his several escapes, crimes and brushes with death during the intervening years.

Perhaps he remembered a short voyage to Van Diemen's Land (later to be renamed Tasmania), the large island off Australia's southern coast. For free men it was a semi-tropical paradise with a natural scenery unsurpassed for its grandeur. A land of verdant valleys, rolling hills and plains, lakes and rivers, bold and rugged mountains with deep gorges and precipitous heights, dramatic seascapes, and forests of 350 feet high blue-gum eucalyptus trees, rivalling in size the giant sequoias of America's California. But for convicts like himself, ruled by the lash and the gallows, it was hell-on-earth. He had endured the agonies of the chain gangs building prisons, roads and bridges, while hampered and cut by manacles on his wrists and feet. He had suffered the taunts of his sadistic military guards, and withstood the agonising pain of frequent floggings at the slightest excuse, during which punishment he had watched with disgust the vicious guard dogs eating strips of his skin as they fell to the ground. And he had found it useless to appeal to the magistrates, the only people who could have helped him had they wished, for they thought all prisoners incapable of reform.

He may have remembered with a wry smile the incident of the stolen cheese in August 1826, which he and three fellow-convicts wolfed down after one of them stole it from a shop while working on a road gang. And they had escaped punishment for the felony through a lack of evidence – they had eaten it! Or he may have recalled the occasion in October 1826 when he was seized red-handed trying to steal a bag of money from a man's pocket, a crime which added yet a further three years to his imprisonment. Then there was the time, ten years later, when he narrowly escaped being hanged for highway robbery. He was, in fact, sentenced to death, but somehow escaped the extreme penalty on this occasion.

He would have had bitter memories of a fellow-prisoner named Mullins who, in the spring of 1845, thwarted Castle's escape attempt from Australia's Port Macquarie prison by leaking his plans to the authorities. Castle, along with three other convicts, William Blackall, Charles Hudson and John Bachelor, had shared their escape plans with Mullins. The conspirators first stole stores to sustain them during their escape, but they were apprehended as they tried to make off in a boat. This time, Castle was sentenced to seven years transportation. William Blackall's penalty was to spend three years in irons on the roads, and Hudson and Bachelor two years in irons on the roads.

Castle finally met his end when he was convicted of what became known as Tasmania's Kangaroo Point murder in the summer of 1852. At his Hobart trial, Castle hotly denied the brutal murder of elderly Billy Hibbert, a recluse who had lived in a hut in the bush. Brief details of the killing were announced in a one-paragraph news item in the *Hobart Town Courier* on 7 April 1852. It read: 'MURDER – An inquest was held at Kangaroo Point ... on view of the body of an aged man familiarly known as 'Billy Hibbert', who lived about a mile from Kangaroo Point. It appears that the deceased was often missing for a few days from his hut, and had been so for several days last past before the inquest. A strong smell coming from the cottage however, the door was broken open, and the old man was found dead, his throat being cut, and his skull being driven in by the blow of an axe. The axe and the knife, covered with blood, were found in the room. A man, who has been considered a companion of the deceased, is in custody.'

Although Castle claimed that he had never met Hibbert, he was found to be wearing the dead man's clothes on his arrest, but to the end he consistently denied being the murderer. He said during his trial: 'I have done many things, but the devil never tempted me to do this ... he never tempted me to imbrue these hands in blood. It is a cruel thing for a man like me, advanced in years, to be charged with a thing of which he is innocent. I can declare in the presence of God, in the presence of this court and the whole court of Heaven, that I am innocent.'

But the unhappy 52-year-old Castle was hanged before a large crowd in front of the Hobart Town gaol. His body was later dissected before burial in the precincts of the prison.

Raines and Wren

The success I encountered in researching Castle's story encouraged me to follow up the exploits of his death cell partners, Samuel Raines and John A. Wren.

Raines, 27, the son of a poor but honest trussmaker who also cleaned guns and pistols to earn extra cash to support his large family, led a blameless life before becoming involved with 19-year-old criminals John Wren and William Elliott.

Elliott, a gang leader, soon talked Raines into pawning a pair of pistols which his father had arranged to clean, and a few days later Elliott redeemed them and used them in a street robbery to relieve a gentleman of a watch worth sixty guineas. The villain then poisoned dogs guarding a large London house, broke in and stole property. But the trio made a fatal mistake when they tried to rob servant John Collins one cold January evening in 1824, as he trudged up to the toll bar in Vauxhall Road, South London, on his way home to his lodgings in Lambeth.

The attempted armed robbery went badly wrong for the thieves, as Collins was later to describe during their trial. He said that a man had approached him and pointed a pistol at his face, threatening to blow out his brains if he didn't hand over his money. Two other robbers then got hold of him, one grabbing him around the waist, and the other holding his left arm, whilst the armed man pressed the pistol against his head.

Despite this, Collins said he struggled free and ran off crying out, 'Murder!' The man with the pistol fired a shot which knocked off Collins' hat without hurting him. The attackers then ran off while Collins shouted 'Stop thief!' after them.

Raines was caught almost immediately by a soldier from the nearby barracks in Rochester Row. Elliott was arrested the next day near Fleet Street. But Wren remained free for a week, although he had dropped his hat while running away and his name was marked inside it.

Telling of Wren's arrest in a brothel, policeman Thomas Pace said he knew him well, and had sought him out after finding the hat. Pace arrested Wren during the early hours of the morning, after breaking down two doors, to find him in bed with a prostitute. On being asked about his hat, Wren jokingly put on a paper cap and said, 'That is all the hat I've got!'

Pace told the court that he found a pistol ankle deep in mud a few yards from where Collins had been attacked.

All three culprits denied the offence, but were sentenced to death. Ironically, because it was his first conviction, ringleader Elliott was later reprieved and transported to Australia. There was no such reprieve for Raines. Our diarist resumes his narrative:

The chapel bell now summoned our attendance. The three unfortunate sufferers were shortly ushered into the condemned pew, I accompanied them to afford every assistance in my power. Poor Castle during the service seemed much affected, and with him his fellow sufferers seemed to sympathize much as did also several other prisoners, while the Rev. Dr Towne delivered an appropriate discourse from 22nd Chapter, 2nd Book of Kings, Verse 1: 'Thus saith the Lord, thou shalt die and not live.'

On the Monday I resumed my visit at nine in the morning and again in the evening after the trying event of a final separation from their friends had taken place. I was joined by Dr Towne who officiated for the Ordinary who was still confined to his room.

After some time in exhortation and prayer, Raines begged me to retire with him to a distant part of the room, when he presented me with a letter directing my attention to the distressed condition of his family who by his crimes had been plunged in to the most trying circumstances.

After this melancholy detail had been presented, and assurance given on my part that the sufferer's request should be duly considered, we joined his fellow sufferers in prayer and other religious exercises, till it was necessary to seek some repose to fit us for the trying events of the coming day. The parting was most interesting, in which the culprits manifested the strongest sense of gratitude and affection, begging as early an attendance as possible on the following day.

At six o'clock in the morning of suffering, I was met by Dr Towne in the lobby at the prison, from whence we then proceeded to the condemned room. We were informed that the sufferers had slept a considerable part of the night, devoting their waking moments to prayer and supplication

On our entrance, we found Raines and Wren preparing themselves for our reception. When they had adjusted their attire, they joined us in devotional exercises, but on their strongly expressing a desire that Castle should be permitted to be present, I immediately went to his cell where he was locked up, and found him in the greatest perturbation; his feelings for the poor sufferers seemed most exquisite and agonizing. He cried out: 'Oh, that I might die with them!'

On my soliciting him to compose his mind, and promising to take him from his cell to join them in prayer and bid them a last adieu, he seemed more composed. When I introduced him, they each embraced each other, mingling their sighs and tears together for a short season.

We then proceeded to the solemn and important work of prayer and supplication, humbling imploring the divine presence and his supporting grace. The sacrament was then administered, in which service they expressed much feeling and devotion, which spirit was fully manifested throughout all their religious exercises till the Sheriffs Officer arrived to demand their immediate appearance.

When the arms of the two sufferers were pinioned, each thanked me for my kind attention. Raines, begging my hand, eagerly pressed it to his lips kissing it most fervently, saying again 'Oh, Mr Baker, do see my poor wife, endeavour to comfort her.'

I said 'Think on that encouraging declaration in scripture, "Leave the fatherless, and let thy widow trust in me."' But I promised to comply with his wish immediately.

We then passed onto the scaffold, the bell tolling the awful note of departure from the fleeting scenes of time, to the more solemn and important events of eternity.

A journalist covered the executions, and his report, part of which I include here, makes interesting reading:

The Sheriff and attendants arrived at the prison shortly before eight o'clock and proceeded to the Press Room where Wren was, dressed in white trousers and blue coat; he appeared careless and firm, joined in prayer on being asked. Raines prayed with a much apparent fervour, and begged of the Sheriff (Sir Peter Laurie) to do something for his wife and children. 'Pity them,' said he 'it is not their fault; had I taken my wife's advice, I should not have been here.'

By eight o'clock, the preparations being completed, they were led to the scaffold. Wren jumped up with much hardihood, and recognizing some person in the crowd, nodded repeatedly, exclaiming with a smile, 'I'm going. Goodbye, God bless you!' Raines was so much affected, that it was found necessary to support him. In a few minutes the drop fell, and they ceased to exist. The crowd assembled was very great.

There is every reason to believe that this was the only act in which Raines was deeply implicated, the news of which so greatly affected his parents, that his mother sunk under the shock, and his father is now confined raving mad in Dean Street workhouse.

Raines's four brothers and sisters are now depending for support on his widow, who has two infant children: they are in the most complete state of destitution, and deserve the commiserations of the public.

A subscription has been set on foot for Raines's widow and family, to which the magistrates of Queen Square, who committed the three wretched men, have liberally contributed, besides ordering a sum of money from the poor box of the office.

More notes from the Diary

A fortnight after the departure of Castle for Australia, Mr Baker had again to offer consolation to three condemned men whose executions had just been confirmed. They were John Hill Wagstaff, John Easterby and William Hill.

Wagstaff, aged 27, an unemployed bachelor, was convicted of passing a forged £250 cheque, his sole offence in an otherwise unblemished career.

Hill, 36, also single and out of work, was caught after trying to buy goods with a forged £5 note from a wary Jewish clothes salesman. He was also convicted of passing other forged money. Hill used a simple but effective technique. Sometimes helped by a female accomplice, he would offer tradesmen and publicans forged fivers for small purchases and then pocket the change. A former policeman, Hill had turned to crime after losing his job for taking a bribe and letting a prisoner escape.

Easterby, 34, a married man, was a confirmed rogue well known to the police as a leading member of a daring gang of London burglars. He was finally convicted after being spotted in an identity parade as one of the villains who had robbed a couple of almost all their belongings in a Christmas Day raid on their home. Baker takes up the story:

Wagstaff was at that time in the infirmary labouring under indisposition. On the fatal news being communicated to him, he bowed with pious resignation, but looked at me with great earnestness and apparent affection while he seized my hand, saying: 'Oh, sir, let me see you as soon as possible. I stand in need of your advice.'

The other sufferers also behaved as became their awful situation and expressed the same wish. Some of the respites [reprieved] manifested much sensibility of feeling, particularly the females who most forcibly called the attention of the messengers of mercy to unite with them in praise for their deliverance.

After having passed through this affecting scene, I called the male respites together, who were by this time removed from their cells to another part of the prison, and addressed them on their miraculous deliverance, most earnestly entreating them to continue steadfast in the practice of those important duties which had been so often pressed upon their attention while under the awful sentence from which they were now happily delivered; they all seemed grateful to receive my admonitions and promised attention thereto.

Before I left the prison, I again visited Wagstaff and walked with him from the infirmary round to the cells, which were now to become for the few remaining hours of his life his gloomy abode. On my retiring, he again in the most affectionate language expressed his gratitude for my attention, saying he should be anxious to see me in the morning, in which expression Easterby and Hill, the two other malefactors, most cordially joined.

From this time I regularly visited them twice a day till the moment of suffering, for which attention they all manifested the greatest gratitude.

There was one incident during my attentions which I think most evidently displayed the sincerity of Wagstaff's repentance and his correct views of the gospel dispensation .... On the Sunday evening previous to the condemned sermon, he said: 'Sir, I have one request to make which if you will have the goodness to attend to, I shall feel particularly obliged.

'We have this day had a gentleman to visit us who has advanced such opinions as I consider dangerous in their tendency, and altho' he came with intent to console, yet I think his declarations are much more calculated to ensnare and mislead than promote either our present peace or eternal happiness.

'He endeavoured to persuade us that if we sincerely believed that Christ came into the world to save sinners, and that he really was the Son of God, we must be saved, let our past, present or future state be what it might, for it was recorded that he that believeth in the Son hath everlasting life, and that he that believeth not in the Son shall not see life; but the wrath of God abideth on him.

'From these portions of scripture he endeavoured to show that we might draw the most certain conclusions respecting our final state and if we did but believe all must be well.'

I said: 'This is a doctrine you are fully sensible I have strongly enforced likewise.'

'Yes, sir,' said he. 'You have most truly done this, and much more than this; for you have practically established it also, for in the expressions of the Saviour you have insisted on the new birth (John 3.3 ... Except a man be born again he cannot see the Kingdom of God). And that those who name the name of Christ are to depart from all iniquity, thus are to become new creatures, old things are to pass away and all things to become new, and that if we have not the spirit of Christ we are none of his, and many other texts of the like nature. But nothing like this dropped from the lips of our new instructor, no penitential feelings, no humility of the heart, no contrition for sin, no sanctifying influence of the Holy Spirit, no Holy Communion with God was once hinted at by him. Therefore, I do not consider him a fit person to attend men circumstanced as we are, and shall feel obliged by your using your interest to prevent any more visits of this nature.'

Hill united in this request and said: 'In the natural course of reasoning, we cannot lose anything by his absence. For you, sir, have clearly pointed out, as much as you can, the absolute necessity of faith in Christ Jesus, which if we have embraced, and I trust we have, surely none of those graces of his spirit which are manifested in the true believers conduct, can be offensive to God; this is impossible. And we are sensible the scriptures bear the fullest testimony that your declarations are right upon this subject.'

I shall only add their request was attended to altho' at the expense of some reproach from the person above alluded to.

The solemnities of the Sunday were most interesting both at the chapel and in the condemned room. As the Ordinary was reading the communion service Wagstaff seemed much affected, and particularly so when the ten commandments were read. On the Ordinary pronouncing 'Remember the Sabbath Day, to keep it holy, etc.,' he burst out in agonizing sobs, covering his face and inclining his head to the table at which time I gently slipped into his hand a scented box with aromatic vinegar, thinking it might relieve him. He with eagerness caught my hand pressing it with marks of the strongest emotion and affection.

The Ordinary's sermon was delivered with much solemnity from the following words, Ezekiel 33.11 'As I live with the Lord God, I have no pleasure in the death of the wicked; but rather that the wicked turn from his ways and live.'

The sufferers withdrew from this service much affected, and during its performance many females were carried out almost in a lifeless state.

After retiring with them from the chapel to the condemned room, I shortly took my leave to get some refreshment, returning again in the afternoon when I was met by several of their near relations who all greeted me with much affection and expressed the greatest gratitude for my attention to the poor sufferers.

On the following day, I paid very requisite attention and was very happy on leaving them at the close thereof in a most composed and serene spirit, notwithstanding the trying conflict of separations from all they held in this world most dear.

I now subjoin the account of the awful time of suffering as given in the newspapers of the day, being strictly correct in every particular.

At this point in his journal, Mr Baker stuck in newspaper clippings, part of which I quote as follows:

About a quarter before eight, Mr Sheriff Whittaker arrived. Easterby was first brought into the room. He was dressed in a black coat and waistcoat, corduroy breeches and black stockings. He appeared to be perfectly sensible to his awful situation, but there was nothing particular in his manner: he appeared quite composed and resigned. When his arms had been pinioned, he went down and sat upon a bench while his companions in guilt went through the same preparation. Hill was next conducted into the room; he had the appearance of having once been a respectable man. He walked perfectly erect, and with a rapid step. He was dressed in black, with a white under-waistcoat, and stood nearly six feet high. On his hands being tied, he complained that the cord was too tight, and it was consequently slackened. He then sat down by Easterby, after shaking hands with several persons near him with much fervour. He said, if he could die in prison he should be more contented, but the public exposure was appalling. Wagstaff was now ushered into the Press Room by Mr Baker, who throughout was constant in his attentions to the wretched sufferer, who appeared more dejected than either of his fellow-criminals. He held his head down and said nothing. He was dressed respectably in black. After these preliminary adjustments were completed, Easterby and Hill took a little water, but Wagstaff declined.

A few minutes of most dreadful suspense now took place ... it was not quite eight o'clock, and the culprits stood gazing at each other, expecting the clock of St Sepulchre's Church to clang the fatal hour. The Sheriffs had their watches in their hands; at last the chime struck upon the ear, and the poor fellows seemed startled. The Rev. Mr Cotton, the Ordinary, preceded by Mr Sheriff Whittaker, led the way to the fatal platform, reciting part of the funeral service as the solemn cavalcade proceeded through the gloomy passages of the gaol.

The same order that had hitherto been observed was maintained on the arrival at the scaffold. Easterby ascended first, and was followed by Hill, whose firmness was conspicuous; he ascended the scaffold without assistance, with a perfect, steady, calm and collected demeanour. While the executioner was fixing the rope, Hill spoke to him several times, as if he was giving directions to be very particular in fitting it to the proper place. Wagstaff was then led up the steps by Mr Baker, who was unremitting in rendering him spiritual consolation and support. When everything was finally arranged, the unhappy men shook hands with each other, and the fatal signal been given, this world closed upon them for ever. Hill died rather hard; the others did not struggle more than ordinarily. After hanging the usual time, the bodies were cut down to be delivered to their friends.

The SURREY COUNTY GOAL, in Horse Monger Lane, near Stones end, Southwark and the new manner of Executing Criminals thereon.

4 Tales from Horsemonger Lane Gaol

No book on London crime would be complete without a mention of Horsemonger Lane Gaol, which was located south of the River Thames at Southwark. It was completed in 1799 in an area infamous since medieval times for its brothels and crime, mainly due to it being outside the jurisdiction of the City of London's legal system. Although it was technically sited in South London in what is now Union Street, the three-storey gaol was built as the new Surrey county prison, housing some 300 inmates. And despite its brief existence in comparison to Newgate – a mere 80 years – it was nevertheless the scene of some memorable executions on its grim scaffold which was erected on the roof of the imposing gateway. A selection of these cases is given below.

An Act of Judicial Revenge

In 1803 the authorities revived an ancient law so that seven conspirators convicted of high treason could be beheaded after being hanged at Horsemonger Lane Gaol. No doubt the hanging and beheading of Colonel Despard and his fellow-conspirators, who plotted the overthrow of the government and the assassination of King George III, was ordered by officials who had become more than a little nervous following the then recent French Revolution and its bloody aftermath. But the plot was in reality little more than a farce, with Despard playing the role of pub orator rather than a serious revolutionary. However, he and some of his cronies were rounded up at a public house in Newington, where it was claimed they had tried to seduce both civilians and low-ranking soldiers into their plot. It was said at their trial – mainly those giving Kings' Evidence to save their own necks – that the villains had planned to seize the Tower of London and steal weapons, take over the Bank of England, and finally kill the King. It seemed they thought their scheme would receive nationwide approval and a general uprising would follow in their favour.

Of the original eleven people charged with high treason, only seven were actually executed. They were Colonel Edward Marcus Despard, Thomas Broughton, John Francis, Arthur Graham, John McNamara, John Wood and James Sedgwick Wratten. Hangman William Brunskill officiated at the hangings assisted by a masked man who carried out the beheadings.

Nature's Protest

Local superstition avers that Horsemonger Lane Gaol executions were accompanied by bad weather, as though Nature itself was protesting at the barbaric practice of hanging. It would be difficult to establish how justified was this belief, but the following two cases certainly occurred during very inclement, but not unseasonable, weather.

The first of these hangings occurred during a snap of intense cold on a dreary January morning in 1829. It was a double execution, and the condemned men were John Jardine, 43, and 24-year-old William Page. Jardine, who complained of the cold, was convicted of trying to poison his wife, whilst Page was found guilty of horse stealing. It must have been an eerie sight indeed, for the grim scaffold was enveloped in a dense fog, and the hangman and his victims were seen by the crowd as mere shadowy puppets in some hideous and deadly sideshow.

A year later almost to the day, it was the turn of 36-year-old William Banks to take his place on the dreaded scaffold. Despite the bitter cold and hurricane-force north-easterly wind, an immense crowd gathered to witness his end. Described as a powerful, athletic man, and the bold and determined leader of a formidable gang of robbers, Banks was convicted of 'a daring burglary and outrage' at the home of the Rev. Warrington in West Molesey, Surrey, a month earlier. After breaking into the house, Banks and his accomplices tied up the clergyman, his lady and their two female servants, and locked them in the cellar before ransacking the house.

The Trades Union Murder

Strange as it may seem, the concept of contract killing by what today are called 'hit men' is not an exclusively modern crime, and one such crime occurred in England as long ago as 1831, in what became known as the Trades Union Murder. The case involved the shooting of mill owner Thomas Ashton, who had the reputation of being a severe employer. In January 1831, at a time of national industrial unrest, Mr Ashton was killed one evening whilst out walking near Marple in Cheshire.

The crime remained unsolved for almost four years until three men were eventually arrested for the killing: James Garside, and brothers Joseph and William Mosley. It was claimed that they had been hired to commit the murder by officials of the Spinner's Union for a fee of £10. William Mosley turned King's Evidence and accused his confederates, saying that a man named Schofield, a well-known union agitator, had handed over the cash to the killers on behalf of the union. The two accused men steadfastly denied the murder and receiving any payment for the crime. Garside and Mosley were nevertheless convicted of the capital offence at Chester Assizes and duly sentenced to death. However, a legal dispute between city and county sheriffs about who was to be responsible for the executions led to the hangings being carried out at London's Horsemonger Lane Gaol. The case naturally aroused much interest, and people travelled from many parts of the country to witness the hangings.

A Doubtful Case

There was also an element of industrial unrest in the case of alleged arsonist James Warner, who admitted setting fire to a mill at Albury, Surrey, in 1830. Warner, aged 30, was illiterate, and although he confessed to the crime there is some doubt as to his guilt: shortly before his execution, a shotgun was fired into the bedroom of the Guildford Workhouse master, and a note was left by unknown criminals who claimed they had committed Warner's crime. The note ended: 'We fired the mill. Starving and firing go together.' The culprits were never caught, and Warner was duly hanged.

There can be no doubt, however, that Warner was guilty of involvement in an earlier crime: he said that two years previously, along with others, he fired a shotgun into a clergyman's house with the intention of killing the occupants; and that crime had indeed remained unsolved until Warner's surprise admission.

A Perverted Act

'Heinous, disgusting and frightful,' were the descriptions of the crime committed by Captain Henry Nicholl in 1833, and women spectators at his Horsemonger Lane Gaol hanging in the August of that year 'by their shouts manifested their abhorrence of the criminal.' Such was the public disquiet engendered that even the pamphlet describing Nicholl's death, printed shortly after his execution, only obliquely referred to the offence for which the 50-year-old former army officer paid the supreme penalty.

Although a multitude of sins, ranging from murder, rape, robbery, appalling child labour, sadism, prostitution and cruelty to animals, were tolerated in some measure in Regency and early Victorian times, one practice was universally condemned – homosexuality! In fact, the perverted act had only one penalty in those unenlightened days, that was death. Sodomites were never reprieved.

Nicholl, who admitted his unnatural relationship with a lad named Lawrence, was not even granted the consolation of a christian burial, for his family ostracised him and refused to receive his body, so that it ended up beneath the dissectionist's blade.

Nicholl had served with distinction in the Peninsular War with the 11th Foot Regiment. He came from a respectable family, his brother being for a time the High Sheriff of Bedfordshire, but he later got into bad company, together with a Captain Beauclerk, and fell into 'evil ways'. Beauclerk, who had faced a similar charge to Nicholl, committed suicide in his Horsemonger Lane Gaol cell, but Nicholl was deprived of the means of his own intended self-destruction by the discovery of a long nail, which was sharpened at the point like a lancet, found in the collar of his coat.

The author of the pamphlet could not help commenting on the distasteful case by opining: 'Thank heavens, the public gallows of Justice in England is very rarely disgraced by the execution of such wretches; but, every person must have observed, with dismay, how greatly the number of diabolical assaults of a similar nature, have lately multiplied in this country.' The trial judge advised Nicholl 'To make all the atonement in his power to an offended God, the few days he had to live; for, he might rest assured, the sentence would not be mitigated.'

Although an unfavourable mood existed against Nicholl in prison, at the end he nevertheless thanked the governor and gaolers for their 'tenderness and humanity', before walking calmly to his death.

A verse was penned by an unknown hand to describe the fate awaiting Nicholl in Hell. It read:

> My thoughts on awful subjects roll
>   Damnation and the dead;
> What horrors seize the guilty soul
>   Upon a dying bed?
> Ling'ring about these mortal shores,
>   She makes a long delay,
> Till, like a flood, with rapid force
>   Death sweeps the wretch away.
> Then swift and dreadful he descends
>   Down to the fiery coast,
> Amongst abominable fiends,

Himself a frightful ghost.
There endless crowds of sinners lie,
And darkness makes their chains;
Tortur'd with keen despair they cry,
Yet wait for fiercer pains.

The Manning Affair

In the autumn of 1849, respectable British citizens were both shocked and outraged to discover that a woman had planned and committed a murder with the help of her husband. This was at a time before women had the vote, and were generally regarded as mere possessions of their menfolk rather than being free-thinking individuals in their own right. The only mitigating factor in the Manning affair, as far as the stolid Victorians were concerned, was the fact that Maria Manning was a foreigner. The attractive Swiss-born redhead, a former lady's maid, had married petty criminal Frederick George Manning after he told her he was due to inherit some property. But nothing came of his anticipated good fortune, and he continued with his employment as a railway guard until he was dismissed on being suspected of involvement in a mail train robbery.

The couple eventually settled down in Bermondsey, South London, and Maria would often be visited at their home by wealthy customs officer Patrick O'Connor, whom she had met some years earlier. Although Frederick Manning did not approve of his wife's affair with O'Connor, he turned a blind eye and even welcomed his rival as a regular guest, on learning that the man had made out a will in Maria's favour. But one evening, after having dined with the Mannings, O'Connor disappeared and his relatives contacted the police. A subsequent search of the Manning home, which had been hurriedly vacated by the couple, revealed O'Connor's body buried in quicklime beneath the kitchen flagstones.

Although the guilty pair had fled, Frederick Manning was soon caught in the Channel Islands where he was well-known, and his wife was apprehended in Edinburgh. She had given both her husband and the police the slip after stealing O'Connor's bonds, valued at several thousand pounds, but she was arrested whilst trying to cash some of them.

Both before and during the trial, the killers tried to blame each other for the murder. In a last-minute admission of guilt, however, Frederick Manning revealed that he and his wife had prepared their victim's grave in the kitchen six months earlier, but that it had taken that long for Maria to find the courage to murder her lover. He said that a wooden shutter had covered the grave, concealed beneath a carpet, which O'Connor had unknowingly walked over many times whilst he was a guest. Manning added that Maria had loaded two pistols and had shot O'Connor in the head with one of them before pointing the other at himself, threatening to shoot him too if he did not help her dispose of the body.

Maria Manning, however, never did admit her part in the crime.

More than 400 policemen controlled the crowd at the hanging of the Mannings at Horsemonger Lane Gaol in November 1849. Hangman William Calcraft untypically performed his duty in an efficient manner, for the couple are said to have died very quickly.

Charles Dickens' description of the behaviour of the crowd who came to witness the hanging is given in Chapter 1. He wrote later: 'I believe that a sight so inconceivably awful as the wickedness and levity of the immense crowd collected at that execution could be imagined by no man, and could be presented in no heathen land under the sun. The horrors of the gibbet and of the crime which brought the wretched murderers to it faded in my mind before the atrocious bearing, looks, and language of the assembled spectators. I do not believe that any community can prosper where such a scene of horror and demoralisation as was enacted this morning outside Horsemonger Lane Gaol is presented at the very doors of good citizens, and is passed by, unknown or forgotten.'

A Justifiable Murder?

It is hard to understand why the case of a man who had cut his mistress's throat in a fit of ungoverned passion should have evoked great public sympathy for the killer, but the conviction of Samuel Wright, father of two young children, led to great efforts by many residents of Lambeth, South London, to save his life in the early days of January 1864. Two petitions bearing more than 3000 signatures were presented to Home Secretary Sir George Grey, requesting a reprieve, but he rejected their pleas. A last-minute appeal to Queen Victoria was also unsuccessful.

Wright had readily admitted slaying his woman, reputedly a violent person of very bad character, with a razor late one night after they had quarelled and she had threatened to leave him. The murderer seems to have subsequently resigned himself to his fate, going uncomplaining to the gallows at Horsemonger Lane Gaol. Although about a thousand policemen attended the execution in case of trouble, most people boycotted the event, the crowd being much smaller than usual. Many houses in the area had their blinds drawn, and shops were closed, in sympathy for the condemned man.

An execution in front of the Debtors' Gate, Newgate, in 1809.

5 By the Debtors' Gate

Avid devotees of true crime stories will know that the dramatic days of highwaymen and Tyburn hangings have been fully covered in countless books, films and television series. But strangely, perhaps, events at Newgate Prison after the abandonment of Tyburn Tree have received scant mention apart from a few notorious, headline-catching cases. This part of my book has been written to redress the balance in some measure. I therefore continue the history of Newgate Prison by recounting a varied but representative selection of cases – ranging from sheep stealing, petty theft, arson, forgery, homosexuality, to robbery, assault and murder – each of which offences merited the death penalty in those turbulent times in London's history. I mention but briefly some of the period's more celebrated crimes, because they have already been covered extensively elsewhere. The period covered is that in which hangings were still public, taking place in front of the Debtors' Gate of Newgate. After 1868 hangings were carried out within the walls of the prison.

A Terrible Punishment

A tale of mutiny, blood, death, escape and capture, aroused the public interest at the Old Bailey trial of Joseph Wall in January 1802. The defendant, reportedly aged between 50 and 60 years, and of a very gentlemanly appearance, faced trial that month for a capital offence committed twenty years earlier. He was charged with having had a soldier flogged to death whilst he was military governor of the British island outpost of Goree, off the coast of Africa, in 1782.

It was the rule in the army that no offences were to be punished except by the sentence of a Courts Martial, but in the case of Sgt Benjamin Armstrong, who died as a result of receiving 800 lashes on the order of Wall, no Courts Martial had been held. Neither was any accuser in the matter heard, nor any defence allowed to be presented.

In fact, the soldier had been summarily flogged by black slaves in a most brutal manner, with the victim dying of his injuries a few days later. The surgeon who had witnessed the whipping, a Mr Ferrick, testified that he was certain that the punishment, which he had thought very severe, had caused the man's death. During the flogging, according to several witnesses, Governor Wall was said to have urged the slaves to do their bloody task by shouting: 'Lay on, you black bastards! Cut him to the heart! Cut him to the liver!'

Denying the allegations, Wall maintained that Sgt Armstrong was punished on the decision of a Courts Martial. Wall claimed the punishment had resulted from mutinous conduct by Sgt Armstrong, who had led a group of soldiers complaining about money owed to them by the island's former head, Governor Adams.

But John Butler, a former Sgt Major at the Goree garrison, said there had been no riot, mutiny or disturbance, nor was any trial held, and his evidence was supported by several other reliable witnesses.

Wall admitted that on the day following the flogging he fled the island to save his own life, and returned to England. Back safely in Britain, he went to stay at Bath 'for the benefit of his health', but two King's Messengers soon arrived to escort Wall to London for interrogation. He travelled with them in a postcoach to Reading where he managed to give them the slip. Wall then walked some sixty miles across country before taking a carriage and escaping to Scotland. Then, before eventually fleeing to France, he met and married a lady from a noble family. At the time of his arrest twenty years later, Wall was the father of a grown-up son.

Wall had lived throughout this period of freedom under the alias of Mr Thompson, including residing under that name in London during the two years prior to his discovery and trial. He finally surrendered himself in the hope that he would be acquitted, and thus freed to follow a normal life. He also wished to claim debts due to him that were in the hands of trustees. But his gamble failed, and he was hanged outside Newgate Prison.

A contemporary press report revealed that: 'The barbarous exultation of the population upon the appearance of Mr Wall on the scaffold resembles the horrid *bravoes* of the French guillotine. It is to be remembered, however, that the inhumanity of the English populace proceeded from their detestation of inhumanity.'

The Hounslow Heath Killers

Hounslow Heath was for centuries a notorious haunt of highwaymen and footpads, who made a living robbing travellers on the road linking London and the West Country. Located on the western fringe of the Greater London area, the road crossed the heath, providing an ideal place for the ambushing of coaches, lone horsemen and travellers on foot. It was a lonely, bleak, wild scrubland with scattered trees and bushes providing cover for such infamous robbers as Dick Turpin, Sixteen-string Jack and Claud Duval. It was not until the late Victorian era that the heath was finally made safe for wayfarers.

It is perhaps not surprising then, that three London thieves thought the heath a perfect place to rob a Mr John Pole Steele while walking from his home in Feltham to nearby Hounslow. The plot was hatched in an East London tavern after the opportunistic villains learned that Mr Steele travelled the route on foot each evening, carrying a considerable amount of cash with him. The plotters, labourers John Holloway and Owen Haggerty, and former coachman Benjamin Hadfield, thought their victim would be easy to deal with and that the rewards would be high. So they put their plan into effect on a cold, moon-bright November evening in 1802.

At first, the robbery went smoothly enough, for Mr Steele readily handed over his money after pleading with the thieves not to harm him. But Haggerty, disappointed at the small sum carried by the man, swore at him and demanded his pocket book. Both Holloway and Haggerty then attacked their unfortunate victim, striking him down with several blows from their cudgels. Hadfield, frightened by the sudden sound of approaching carriage wheels, deserted his companions and fled towards London. As he ran, he heard repeated cries of 'Murder!' The runaway's partners caught up with him about an hour later. They called him a 'white-livered coward' and refused him a share of the proceeds of their bloody crime.

They met again the next day, when Hadfield noticed that Holloway was wearing a strange hat and boots. On examining the hat, he discovered it was marked with the name Steele in the lining. He pointed this out to Holloway, who later filled the hat with stones and threw it into the river from Westminster Bridge. The trio then parted company and went their several ways, their guilt remaining undiscovered for some four years.

There the matter may have rested, and perhaps remained a mystery for all time, but in September 1806, Hadfield committed a further crime, and was sentenced to transportation for seven years after being convicted of grand larceny. A short while later, on board a prison hulk near Portsmouth, Hadfield became ill. Thinking he was dying, he said he wanted to make a death-bed confession to clear his guilty conscience. He then told the authorities what he knew about Mr Steele's murder (and later pointed out the scene of the crime).

Holloway and Haggerty were soon traced and arrested, but they denied any knowledge of the crime. They claimed that they were complete strangers to each other. But officers hid behind a partition at the police station and eavesdropped on the men's conversation, which they later alleged revealed their involvement in the murder. At the subsequent trial, Hadfield gave King's evidence and testified against them. Other witnesses were also called to confirm the previous friendship between the prisoners. Both were convicted and sentenced to death, but Hadfield was pardoned and freed after the trial.

Holloway and Haggerty were hanged outside Newgate Prison. Holloway's final words on the gallows were: 'Innocent! Innocent, gentlemen! No verdict! No verdict! Innocent, by God!'

A tremendous crowd gathered for the hangings, and about thirty men, women and children were trampled to death by the mob, and some fifteen others were seriously injured. The spectators' bodies were displayed in the nearby St Bartholomew's Hospital, St Sepulchre's Church and the Swan public house, to await identification by relatives.

A Woman of the Town

With Holloway and Haggerty on the gallows was the Marylebone knife murderess, Elizabeth Godfrey. It was a simple domestic dispute that led to the killing of London coachman Richard Prince by Godfrey, a prostitute who became a resident in the same Marylebone lodging house that was the home of Mr Prince and his common-law-wife Emily Bisset, in December 1806. One of Godfrey's clients complained that she had robbed him of 18 shillings, so Mr Prince called the watch (police), and the prostitute was arrested and detained overnight.

Two days later, on the Christmas Day afternoon, while Mr Prince and his lady were having tea, Godfrey knocked on their door and asked to speak with Mr Prince. Agreeing, the man went to talk with his neighbour outside on the landing. What happened next was dramatically described in court by Emily Bisset. She said that she had heard Godfrey complain to Mr Prince about his calling the law, and then the prostitute had exclaimed: 'Take that!' Mr Prince then reeled back into the room with a knife protruding from his left eye. He immediately removed the bloody weapon and threw it to the floor, declaring: 'I'm a dead man!'

The landlord, Mr William Scott, heard the disturbance and ran upstairs. He quickly summed up the situation and asked Godfrey how she could have done such a wicked thing to a fellow-creature. She replied: 'It served him right!'

Help was called, and Mr Prince was rushed to the Middlesex Hospital where he died three weeks later.

In court, Godfrey claimed that she had been beaten by the deceased, whereupon she ran to her room, caught up a knife in the dark, not knowing what it was, and struck Mr Prince without intending to kill him. But the jury did not believe her story, and she was condemned to hang.

Death of a Madman

In our own enlightened times, Britain's citizens are safe from punishment for their crimes committed during periods of insanity. But this was not always so under British law. A case in point is that of 65-year-old Thomas Bowler, who in 1812 tried to kill a neighbour whilst suffering from paranoid delusions following head injuries received in a fall from a horse.

Bowler, a wealthy farmer who lived at Alperton in suburban west London, had for many years got on well with his farming neighbour William Burrows. But following Bowler's accident, the injured man showed a sudden enmity for his former friend, and even threatened to kill him. The intended victim laughingly ignored the menacing warning, attributing it to Bowler's new eccentricity. But early one bright May morning, as Burrows was driving his chaise-cart to town, Bowler stepped out from behind a tree brandishing a blunderbuss. He called out: 'Damn your eyes! Take that!' and fired. Witnesses then saw Bowler throw his weapon in a ditch, mount his mare and gallop off.

The victim, wounded in he head, neck and back, fell forward in the cart across the shafts, and the terrified horse bolted. Fortunately for Burrows, his wounds were not fatal and he eventually recovered.

Sadly, though the trial jury heard that Bowler had been medically judged insane at the time of the shooting, he was nevertheless convicted and hanged for his 'crime'.

A Political Killing

Although political killings are a common event in some parts of the world, the assassination of statesmen in Britain is virtually unknown. The exception to the rule, however, was the fatal shooting of Prime Minister the Rt. Hon. Spencer Perceval in the lobby of the House of Commons in May 1812.

Perceval, a former Solicitor General, Attorney General and Chancellor of the Exchequer, became the country's premier in 1809. He was murdered by bankrupt businessman John Bellingham, who claimed he had been denied justice by the British establishment. Indeed, Bellingham boasted that he had killed Perceval as a deliberate act of revenge and as a warning to the government to heed the complaints of its citizens.

The killer was described as a 'profligate adventurer', whose expertise in commercial transactions had early in life procured the confidence of some respectable business houses engaged in the Russia trade. Bellingham then went to Russia, drew bills on his principals to the amount of £2000, never made any shipments, and squandered the cash. But while he was preparing to leave Russia for England he was arrested for private debts.

Denying this, Bellingham claimed he had been unjustly treated, and said he spent the next two years having a terrible time in various Russian prisons, being continually switched from dungeon to dungeon , and fed mostly on bread and water. He said he was frequently marched through the streets under military guard alongside vicious criminals, degraded and insulted until he was finally able to make his case known. But his troubles, he complained, were not even then resolved, and he had endured much further suffering before his eventual release and return to England.

Whatever the truth behind Bellingham's grievances, whether his claims were real or imaginary, one thing is certain. The tormented man became obsessed with his cause, and increasingly bitter at the lack of any official concern at his plight. The matter overpowered his mind, festering in his thoughts, driving him to an uncontrollable anger which found its violent outlet in murder, thereby ensuring his own destruction.

In court he denied the murder charge, despite the fact that he had committed the deed before witnesses, and was arrested at the scene of his crime. Although many thought him insane, Bellingham was considered fit enough to stand trial, and was quickly convicted. The father of two small children, he was executed outside Newgate Prison in pouring rain, and his body was handed over to surgeons for dissection.

Justice or Judicial Murder?

The Elizabeth Mary Fenning case had the classic ingredients of a stage melodrama – the attempted murder of an influential London family, sexual innuendo, vicious lies, wicked employer, evil judge and an innocent servant girl cruelly killed in order to hide a family scandal. Acted out on stage with a last-minute happy ending the events would have pleased an audience, but in real life they marked a terrible tragedy.

It was in the spring of 1815 that 20-year-old Eliza, an Irish girl, was employed as a trainee cook at the home of Mr Robert Gregson Turner, a law stationer in London's Chancery Lane. Other occupants of the house which comprised a shop, office and home, were Mr Turner's wife Charlotte, housemaid Sarah Peer and two teenage male apprentices.

Some three weeks after starting her job, Eliza, reputedly an attractive and intelligent young woman, was threatened with dismissal by her mistress who had seen her go into the young men's room partly undressed. It was this trivial incident which was later claimed to be the motive behind her supposed attempt to poison the Turner family.

A few days after Eliza had been reproved, apprentice Roger Gadsdell reported that a paper containing arsenic kept for poisoning rats was missing from an unlocked office drawer.

A fortnight later, Eliza, now anxious to please and show what a good cook she was, asked to be allowed to make dumplings for dinner, a request she had often previously made in vain. But to her delight, Mrs Turner finally agreed because a brewer had delivered some yeast to the house. The usual practice had been for the cook to buy ready-made dough in order to save time and labour.

Eliza, acting on Mrs Turner's instructions, first prepared a pie for the apprentices and took it to the local bakery for cooking at about 11.30 am, returning at noon. When she returned to the empty kitchen where the dumpling ingredients had been left untended, she was joined by her mistress who told her how to prepare the dough and then left her to get on with the work. Eliza used milk provided by housemaid Sarah Peer in preparing the food and sauce.

Sarah and the apprentices ate their pie and suffered no ill effects from the meal. But Mr and Mrs Turner, Mr Turner's father and Eliza (she ate her meal in the kitchen as was the custom with servants) all became very ill after eating the dumplings. They each suffered severe pains, swellings and vomiting for several hours. Apprentice Roger Gadsdell, who had helped himself to a small piece of leftover dumpling and sauce, also became ill.

Surgeon John Marshall was quickly called in and he diagnosed arsenical poisoning, an opinion supported by the discovery of what was thought to be arsenic in the remains of the dumplings.

Eliza was charged, convicted and hanged solely on the circumstantial evidence that she had prepared the poisoned food, despite the fact that other members of the household had equal opportunity to both steal and administer the poison.

So what is one to make of the case? Could the poison have got into the food by mistake – a doubtful conclusion when one considers the missing arsenic? Or was housemaid Sarah Peer the guilty party? Significantly, apart from one apprentice, she was the only other person not to have eaten the tainted dumplings. She also served the victims with their meal.

After all these years, of course, one can only speculate on a solution to the mystery. After studying a transcript of the trial, I cannot understand how any jury could have convicted Eliza on the evidence, or rather the lack of it, presented at a very brief proceedings. The case was obviously a complete travesty of justice, and as an earlier writer has aptly put it 'her defence was shamefully conducted'. In fact, her defence was limited to her being allowed only to state her innocence and produce four character witnesses. Little, apparently, was made of the fact that Eliza herself ate some of the poisoned food and became violently ill along with the others – hardly the act of a poisoner!

Her case, no doubt, was also hindered by being heard before the infamous hanging judge, Sir John 'Black Jack' Silvester, Recorder of London, who, it was said, referred to his trial calendars as his 'bills of fare' and who was considered by many to be a rough, violent, un-feeling man.

This unsavoury affair was investigated and to some degree exposed by the celebrated writer, publisher and bookseller William Hone (1780–1842). Hone lived with his large family in a house in the Old Bailey, and from his window he often witnessed public executions outside Newgate Prison. It was after seeing Eliza meet her premature death and being aware of the popular belief in her innocence, that he determined to get to the bottom of the matter. He published the dis-turbing results of his investigations in a pamphlet, the conclusions of which, significantly, were never to be challenged by the powerful people he had criticized.

The bookseller found the situation far from being the simple, straightforward case that was presented before the jury, and that the dice had been well and truly loaded against Eliza from the outset.

Hone discovered that at the very moment Eliza was writhing in agony from the effects of the poison, her employer's father, Haldebart (Olibart) Turner, had refused her father entry to the house with the excuse that his daughter was not at home. He did not have the courage to address the man himself, but instead passed on his blatant lie through the housemaid. In fact, Eliza's parents did not find out about the attempted poisoning until their daughter was being ques-tioned by magistrates the next day.

Although one can never know for certain why Turner was so hos-tile towards Eliza, it is reasonable to surmise that he was trying to hide a family scandal, for according to Hone: 'Mr Turner had himself, previous to the trial, been informed of a circumstance in his own family, which, had it been known to the jury who tried Eliza Fenning, would doubtless, notwithstanding the array of prosecution evidence against her, have procured her acquittal.' Indeed, suspicion was later to fall upon a nephew of Turner's, who some thought attempted the murders through revenge for being kept short of money.

Another theory which was popularly believed at the time was that Robert Gregson Turner himself was the culprit. A rumour quickly spread throughout the neighbourhood that in a bout of mental ill-ness he had bought the arsenic and threatened to kill off his family.

For some strange reason, Haldebart Turner received a visit from judge 'Black Jack' Silvester following Eliza's conviction – not what one would have expected under the circumstances. And thereafter, Turner adamantly refused to sign any petition for mercy, claiming that he was following Silvester's advice.

Hone also found that there was a campaign of smears spread by Turner regarding Eliza and her family, both before and after the execution. Hone wrote later: 'Mr. O. Turner, with the opportunity of knowing them to be false, entertained horrible reports against Eliza Fenning, before her execution, charging her with having attempted to murder families in which she had lived before she went into his.' Hone added that shortly before Eliza's burial, Turner got a Newgate prison officer to criticize her father's conduct as a parent, and publicised this criticism in both newspapers and handbills. Turner also produced a letter alleging Eliza's 'murderous acts in other families'. The basis of this claim, revealed Hone, lay in the 'idle gabble of an ignorant grocer, and the news of a barber; and that the same were wholly false and untrue.' Hone also observed that Turner had cast as bad a light as possible on Eliza during his evidence at the trial.

In a very brief report commenting on the outcome of the trial, a journalist said that after the return of the jury with a guilty verdict, 'The unhappy culprit instantly fell into a fit, screamed and cried aloud most bitterly, and was carried from the dock in a state of insensibility.'

So much public disquiet was created by the verdict that no less than two separate reviews of the case were held by the Lord Chancellor on the day before Eliza's execution. But there was to be no reprieve. Eliza, together with two men who had been condemned to death for other crimes, went to the gallows on the morning of 26 July 1815. She wore what was to have been her wedding dress and cap. Eliza persisted in her innocence to the end, and as she approached the fatal platform, she told Newgate Prison Ordinary, the Rev. Dr Horatio Cotton: 'Before the Just and Almighty God, and by the faith of the Holy Sacrament I have taken, I am innocent of the offence with which I am charged.'

Eliza's father bought her body from executioner John Langley, and the funeral was held at the Church of St George the Martyr, Southwark, where an estimated crowd of 10,000 people saw her laid to rest.

Today, a busy road separates the church from what remains of the larger part of the graveyard. Although the tombstones have been removed, and the graves themselves lie beneath a neat lawn beside a modern office block, the small park has an air of tranquility which provides a peaceful haven amid the hustle and bustle of space-age London.

And what became of the trial judge, the infamous Sir John Silvester? He died in his sleep, aged 76, after a night of drinking and carousing with the Duke of York and some of his cronies, seven years after Eliza's cruel end. His obituary was obviously carefully worded, for it chose to excuse his unpopularity with the common people by noting: 'He was a truly loyal subject of his Sovereign, and ever anxious to uphold the best interests of his country, and the rights, privileges and immunities of this great metropolis (London). This conduct he always pursued fearlessly, and without disguise; which not unfrequently drew upon him the calumny of envenomed factious minds, and roused the lurking envy of others ...'

Men of Blood

The loathsome use of *agents provacateurs* (those who encourage others to commit crimes so that they may betray them and collect a reward) is still practised today, as it has been for many years. In Regency times, the scoundrels who conspired in this fashion were called 'men of blood' and their financial rewards described as 'blood money' . They were usually police officers, and occasionally government officials, seeking both quick cash and promotion, although some professional criminals were sometimes instigators.

The problem became so acute that in the autumn of 1816 the authorities in London took stern measures, resulting in several trials of men of blood. In September of that year occurred the most famous of such cases. In the dock were *agents provocateurs* Michael Power, John Pelham and Thomas Brock, who had tricked three Irishmen into unwittingly help produce counterfeit coins, before betraying them to the police. The naïve 'coiners' were caught in the act, tried and condemned to death. But luckily, shortly before they were due to hang, an astute police investigation discovered the truth and the bewildered Irishmen were pardoned. The three victims, together with other witnesses, later gave evidence against the men of blood, who were duly convicted and punished. During their trial, the Attorney General said the villains had almost sacrificed the lives of three innocent men 'to satisfy their own atrocious love of lucre.'

The Lord Mayor of London, Matthew Wood, felt so strongly about the matter that he helped raise funds which enabled the Irishmen to return home and set themselves up as farmers.

September 1816 also saw the conviction of rogue policeman Benjamin Johnson for his part in a burglary more than a year earlier. Johnson had encouraged William Baxter, a young man, to break into a London house and steal goods and cash. And although the policeman had planned the raid and stood guard during its progress, he immediately arrested his partner-in-crime after the incident. He claimed that Baxter was 'the greatest rogue on earth', and that he had arrested him in the discharge of his duty. Baxter was duly convicted, and Johnson received a £10 reward.

Baxter's father, however, accused Johnson of entrapping his son, and the officer replied: 'If I gave a pistol into a man's hand to shoot another, is he to do it because I told him?' But reliable witnesses proved collusion between the two offenders, and Johnson was eventually punished for his capital crime. He pleaded with the judge for a speedy execution because of the harsh treatment he was enduring from his fellow-convicts in Newgate Prison.

Two other similar cases of police officers convicted of enticing others to commit burglaries were proved that month.

During the following month, the editor of *The Times* revealed a men-of-blood plot involving a Jew named Solomon and several police officers. A news report, headed More Conspiracies, declared that Solomon chose his victims from amongst the Russians, the Maltese, Germans and Irish, as well as the English. The story went on:

His plan was to station himself somewhere in the neighbourhood of the Tower, and, when he saw a sailor who had spent all his money, or been robbed of it, he would with pretended humanity give him a [forged] shilling, or in cases of extreme necessity, a 3s. token. The first place to which his necessities would lead the wretch to whom his bounty was extended, would be the baker's shop, or the eating house; but as soon as the supposed value was tendered, a police officer started into his presence, seized the money, marked it, and handcuffed the poor creature that offered it. Upon being brought before a magistrate, the story was just such as is usually told, and no suspicion excited.

In other instances this ingenious Jew, without pretending to be influenced by any compassionate motives, would merely propose to poor tattered sailors to purchase certain articles at a slop-shop, or marine stores warehouse, with a promise to give them a drink for their trouble. Upon proceeding to execute their commission, they were scented by the officer, who was sure to let them go just as far as was necessary to make them guilty in the eye of the law upon his testimony.

The Lord Mayor's deep concern at the matter prompted him to spend a whole Sunday at Newgate, where together with an advisor he took the depositions of eighteen inmates who claimed that they had been framed by Solomon. Bank officials confirmed that police officers involved in the arrests had received £10 rewards for each conviction.

I was unable, unfortunately, to find any report to show that Solomon and the criminal police officers were ever brought to justice.

At the Scene of the Crime

The last offender to be executed at the scene of his crime was Royal Navy sailor John Cashman. He was hanged in 1817 in Skinner Street, Clerkenwell, in front of Mr Beckwith's shop, a gunsmiths which he had 'attacked and plundered' during a street disturbance. He had been drinking heavily prior to the incident.

By his own account, Cashman was born at sea and for a long time he lived in America before joining the British navy. His mother and two brothers settled near Cork in Ireland. His naval superior officers reported that Cashman had a good record, that he had fought bravely on various occasions, was wounded several times and had received head injuries.

Cashman, referring to his pending execution, told officials that he disliked the idea of being taken to the Skinner Street scaffold in a cart. He did not want to be taken through the streets like a vagrant or a common robber. He said that if he had been a felon or a murderer, then he would not have minded such common exposure. Mr Beckwith, the gunsmith, was equally anxious that the hanging should not happen outside his shop, and he twice unsuccessfully asked the Secretary of State to have the execution carried out elsewhere.

But Cashman seems finally to have taken the whole matter in his stride. Indeed, after sentence, he affected an air of amused bravado. On remarking on his forthcoming end, he said that he had often faced the enemy amidst a shower of balls, and with the devil before him, without shrinking, and did not now fear to face his God. But as he left the prison he exclaimed: 'I wish a 44-pounder would now come and cut me in two, rather than I should go into the hands of Jack Ketch.'

A newspaper report, describing his last moments, revealed that: 'Everything being in readiness, the melancholy procession moved forward. The criminal, as he passed along, nodded to the crowd, and continued to inveigh in loud language against the injustice of his punishment, declaring that he had done nothing but what he was driven to, and that he had been robbed by merchants, as well as government of his due. "This," said he, "is what brought me here. I always fought for my King and country, and this is my end."'

A Promising Start

Great public sorrow was expressed that same month at the execution for forgery of 19-year-old John Vartie. Born in Westmorland of respectable parents, Vartie was later described as being a gentle and decent young man. He proved an accomplished scholar at an early age, becoming adept at Latin, Greek, and mathematics. He was employed successively as tutor to a noble family, a school usher, and a clerk with a Gravesend bank.

In a sketch of his life which he wrote in the death cell at Newgate Prison, Vartie confessed to having a romantic imagination. He claimed he had often passed his time alone in solitary places enjoying imaginative contemplation of fictional scenes of adventure amid ruined castles, rocks, precipices and cascades roaring through echoing groves. But then, he revealed, he developed a sudden fascination for reading licentious and profligate books. And this led to his seeking bad company and to casting aside his religious beliefs. His reading, he stated later, had filled him with 'unnatural ideas and a disgust with common life'. He also became restless and ambitious, rapidly heading for his downfall by finally committing the forgery for which he was condemned.

A few lines in the *Maidstone Gazette* recorded that Vartie was buried by friends at Milton graveyard, and that a public subscription was arranged to raise cash to erect a stone to his memory.

An Unnatural Crime

Child murder is no doubt the most controversial of crimes. By its very nature it is a subject which arouses atavistic feelings of horror and revulsion in even the most indifferent of people. And it reaches into the hearts and minds of many of the most hardened criminals, members of an ungodly brotherhood which, although ever ready to break society's rules, abhors this unnatural act, and has its own methods of punishing the guilty.

Yet there arise from time to time cases where some sympathy may be felt for the offenders. Mercy killers, for instance, or people like Sarah Perry who, although a mother who killed her own infant, was perhaps herself a victim of the culture and time in which she lived.

Appalling double standards of behaviour were the norm in Regency England. Life was wonderful for the rich and successful: they could get away with almost anything provided it could be conveniently concealed from the public eye, and the influential parents of illegitimate children could easily hide the births of such offspring by off-loading them for a financial consideration. But for the unfortunate women who were both unmarried and poor it was quite a different matter. If they were domestic servants, as many were, then pregnancy usually resulted in both loss of job and home, for illegitimacy at that time was considered almost a crime, and employers seldom allowed disgraced servants to remain under their roofs. It is not surprising then that back street abortions were rife, and that some women were even driven to murdering their newly-born children.

So it was in the case of Sarah Perry, who in February 1817 worked as a cook in a house in Manchester Street, near London's famous Baker Street. Others living in the house, as well as the master and mistress, were the maid Charlotte Armstrong and footman William Roots.

The trouble started on a cold winter night as Perry, who passed as a married woman, prepared for bed. As was often the custom in Regency times, the cook and the maid shared a bed. As Perry prepared for bed, the maid remarked that her body appeared very large. The cook brushed this observation aside by saying that it was due to the thickness of her clothing.

A few nights later the maid was awakened during the early hours of the morning by Roots the footman, who asked her to go downstairs with him because the cook was ill in the scullery. Without pausing to dress, she immediately went down to the kitchen. It was quite dark, and the cook remained in the scullery which was divided from the kitchen by a thin partition. Although she could not see Perry, Charlotte Armstrong asked what was the matter. The cook replied: 'I am very ill. I have a great pain in my bowels.' And she begged the maid to keep out of the scullery.

At Perry's request, the maid left a light in the kitchen, and then went upstairs to her mistress who had rung the bell. She remained upstairs for about ten minutes before returning. But Perry pushed her back out of the kitchen and bolted the door, telling her to go back to bed and that she herself would soon follow.

After waiting some time, the maid eventually returned to her room, to be followed by Perry at about 6.30 am. The cook arose shortly before 8.00, and she was followed downstairs by the maid some fifteen minutes later.

At about 10.00 am that same morning, the inquisitive maid searched the scullery and saw enough to convince her that the cook had given birth there. She immediately told her mistress of her suspicions and a Bow Street officer was called in. A subsequent search revealed a child's body in the coal hole. The female baby had been concealed in a bundle and hidden beneath coal. Its mouth was packed with cloth which had choked it.

Perry later admitted that she had hidden the birth for fear of losing her job. But she neither confirmed nor denied killing the baby. The wretched woman was quickly convicted of wilfully murdering her child, and she was hanged three days later. A newspaper report recorded that 'she was launched into eternity in the presence of a greater concourse of women that we ever remember to have seen assembled on any similar occasion.'

It is interesting to compare the Sarah Perry case with that of 24-year-old child killer, Catherine Welch, eleven years later in April 1828. Although one may possibly have some vestige of sympathy for Perry, such feelings would be entirely misplaced for Welch, because she quite cold-bloodedly planned and carried out the cruel murder of her thriving baby.

During her trial, Welch frequently protested her innocence, but she finally broke down and confessed a few hours before her execution. She revealed that about a year earlier she had lived at a public house in London's City Road, and became involved with a waiter there named Hayes. She quickly became pregnant by the man and had to leave her job. Some two month later, she met and married a man named Welde. But her quickly acquired husband soon deserted her, leaving her destitute, on learning that she was going to have another man's child.

Welch then looked up her lover Hayes, who visited her at Feltham several times before the birth of their baby. The child was born in good health. She again sent for Hayes following her confinement, seeking his advice, claiming that her husband was determined not to live with her again.

Following his visit, Welch murdered her infant in a particularly brutal manner: when its body was examined by a doctor after being discovered in a water-filled ditch at Turnham Green, Chiswick, the baby boy was found to have been strangled, had received head injuries, and its eyes had been gouged out.

Welch denied throughout that the dead child was hers. Instead, she claimed that after being delivered of her own baby it soon died of natural causes. But, she insisted, she could not remember where it had been laid to rest, or the identity of the couple whom she said had taken it away for burial. And she added ironically: 'I am as innocent as a baby unborn.'

However, she finally admitted that it was after having had a talk with her lover that she had decided to kill her baby. After her trial, Welch seemed calmly to accept the justice of her fate. She declared herself ready to suffer her punishment, even if it should prove a thousand times as severe as that which awaited her, for she was sure that God would forgive her. But according to a journalist who covered her execution, the unfortunate woman died hard. Her death struggles were described as very great, no doubt due to her 'being a rather fine young woman of a stout and particularly healthy appearance.' Her body was later handed over to surgeons for dissection.

The Cato Street Conspiracy

I shall not dwell long on this famous case, as it is already so well known. However, this conspiracy to assassinate the entire British cabinet whilst attending a dinner is interesting in that the plot was almost certainly hatched by one George Edwards, a notorious 'man of blood'.

Edwards befriended a London-based group of hot-headed radicals, and they together evolved a crazy scheme, which they believed would lead to a general revolution with themselves heading a provisional government. Edwards also gave them practical support in the form of cash and weapons.

The main conspirators were Arthur Thistlewood, aged about 50, a professional gambler and political agitator, who was described as being 'tall, thin, and possessed of a gloomy countenance'. Next came 45-year-old Richard Tidd, who made a precarious living by enlisting in various military regiments and promptly deserting on receiving his cash bounties. Then there was former Portsmouth butcher, James Ings, who, although impoverished, managed to run a coffee shop in Whitechapel where he also sold political pamphlets, a fact which prompted the others to invite him to join their cause. Although he was baptised in 1794, Ings was claimed to be aged between 50 and 60 at the time of his execution in 1820. Lesser members of the group, backed up by a team of others, were Jamaican William Davidson, a 35-year-old failed businessman who had become involved in a sexual scandal, and John Thomas Brunt, aged 38, a skilled London boot maker.

The schemers held their secret meetings in a disused stable loft in Cato Street off London's Edgware Road, where they also stored weapons and made hand grenades.

At the critical moment, the authorities were tipped off (the identity of the informer was not reported) and the stable was raided at night by Bow Street officers, one of whom, Richard Smithers, was run through with a sword and killed by Thistlewood, who then made his escape in the darkness. But his freedom was short-lived, for his hiding place was revealed by an informer and he was caught unawares in bed.

Thistlewood, Tidd, Ings, Brunt and Davidson soon appeared in court charged with high treason, and some of their former colleagues gave King's Evidence against them, which secured their convictions.

The State was determined to make an example of the guilty men in order to deter other would-be rebels at a time of great social unrest in Britain's history. The official revenge came in the form of the convicted men being publicly beheaded after their hangings outside

Newgate Prison in May 1820.

Significantly, although a reward of £100 was offered for the capture of George Edwards, he was never caught, and he reputedly lived out his days undetected 'in some far-off country'.

To Die with Dignity

It was a varied and unrelated group of six which shuffled onto Newgate's grim gallows on a certain cold December morning in 1820. Their demeanour, according to the newspapers of the day, was unique for people about to die in this fashion. So much so that an onlooker recorded that 'the appearance of all of them was much more respectable than is generally seen in such a situation, and their behaviour on the scaffold highly exemplary; they joined in their devotions with great fervour.'

Just who were these felons who assembled to face death together? And what were their crimes? They were: Joseph Ellinger and George Edwards, convicted of highway robbery; Thomas Webb, a self-employed bricklayer who committed sacrilege; ex-army officer Thomas Fuller Harnett, 27, found guilty of forging a Bill of Exchange; and John Madden, aged 20, and 43-year-old Sarah Price, both caught passing counterfeit banknotes.

Joseph Ellinger, aged 21, described as being a smart-looking young man, was convicted after he had hustled and robbed a man of £41 in London's Hackney Fields. George Edwards, 27, was also charged with robbery after assaulting and stealing property from a man in Chapel Street, near the Edgware Road. He was quickly caught by a passer-by who witnessed the crime. Both robbers were of previous good character.

Thomas Webb, age unknown, who had a wife and four children to support, broke into Enfield Church late one night and stole 600 yards of black cloth and a surplice. Although he denied the offence, claiming he was at home when the break-in occurred, he was condemned for sacrilege.

The evidence against John Madden was very scant indeed. Caught in the company of youthful companions who were strongly suspected of passing forged £1 notes, Madden was condemned solely on suspicion of his having swallowed a forged note. No forgeries were found on him, so it is difficult to understand how he could have been fairly convicted. It was popularly believed that he was hanged because he refused to admit the allegations against him.

Sarah Price was convicted of passing a forged £1 note, a temptation it was claimed she had found hard to resist. Shortly before her own arrest her son was transported to the colonies for dealing in bad notes, and although Price admitted passing several other forged notes, she had never previously been caught. Despite her husband's warning, she tried to buy a pair of shoes with a dubious banknote, but the forgery was immediately spotted and Price was apprehended. A reporter covering her execution said of her: 'This woman exhibited a degree of fortitude beyond anything than can be expressed.'

Thomas Fuller Harnett, or Captain Harnett as he was popularly known, was hanged for forging a £20 Bill of Exchange. Born into a wealthy Irish family, Harnett served as a Lieutenant in the army for some years, before turning to a life of dissipation, resulting in his capital offence and early violent death.

A Rake's Progress

Samuel Hayward was a living example of the main character in William Hogarth's series of paintings titled The Rake's Progress (1735), portraying the seamier side of London life. Living as he did in the reign of the dissipated monarch King George IV, Hayward may be truly termed a Regency dandy, and his lifestyle certainly matched that label.

In less than a decade, Hayward, the ambitious and gifted son of a humble currier, made a meteoric rise in life, from being a tailor's assistant to becoming the confidant of some of London's top people. He carefully engineered his upward mobility by first becoming a waiter at the York Coffee House, a meeting place of the influential near London's Royal Exchange. There, his genteel qualities were soon spotted by historian Dr Pugh Gueston, who hired him to research material for his book History of London. It was during his six months stint with the good doctor that the intellectually brilliant Hayward mastered both the French and Italian languages, which it was later claimed he spoke with great fluency. He also became proficient in music and dancing, and acquired the manners so essential in polite society.

Hayward then transferred his loyalties to a Captain Blanchard, with whom he travelled for about nine months before deserting him to take up a career as a professional gambler in London's West End gaming clubs. He shared his good fortune with some of the city's most notorious courtesans, at the same time worming himself into the confidence of several prominent and respectable London families. His progress in high society was achieved through his masterly acquisition of the distinguished graces of the accomplished English gentleman.

But sudden gambling losses led Hayward to turn to crime in an effort to maintain his expensive way of life, with a fatal result.

In November 1821 Hayward found himself in court accused of stealing plate, jewellery and linen from a house near Clarendon Square, St Pancras. He was described in a press report as being 'a young man, elegantly dressed in black and of a prepossessing person'. But his youth, charm, appearance and superior manners could not prevent him from being convicted of the capital crime of burglary, and he was hanged alongside Joseph South, aged 16, condemned for passing forged banknotes, and Anne Norris, who died for robbery.

Shortly before his premature death, Hayward entertained some forty other Regency dandies who visited him in the death cell at Newgate Prison.

Asked how he felt at the prospect of being executed, Hayward told Mr Sheriff Venables: 'As a man ought to feel who has violated the laws of God and his country.'

All for Beauty

The joint hanging of three unfortunate men in the autumn of 1821 was marked by the revival of a superstitious and gruesome custom. Shortly before the dead bodies were cut down, several young women emerged from the crowd, climbed upon the gallows, and rubbed their bodies with hands of the corpses. The belief at the time was that immediately after the execution a dead man came out in a 'death sweat' which had miraculous healing powers and was particularly efficacious in removing facial spots, warts, and other body blemishes. And so ingrained was this ridiculous notion that normally respectable, intelligent and modest women would remove most of their clothing before the gawking crowd to carry out the distasteful ritual.

The men who died on that occasion were William Thomson, 18, George Lee, age unknown, and 40-year-old Thomas Patmore.

A woman swoons as she receives the death sweat from a corpse's hand in an attempt to cure her bodily blemish.

Thomson, who had mugged a man in the street, was described by a journalist as a 'miserable youth, who was most distressingly ignorant and even stupid.' The lad had no living relatives, and when his employment ceased through his master's lack of business, he was turned loose on to the London streets, where hunger and poverty soon drove him to crime. Lee, who was Jewish, was convicted of passing a forged £5 note. Thomas Patmore was condemned for the attempted murder of Lt. Gen. William Eden, whom he stabbed in the chest with a long butchers' knife at his home in London's fashionable Hanover Square. Patmore, who had served the officer for some nine years, claimed his victim had seduced his wife, so he had tried to kill him in revenge. But Patmore's wife throughout refused to confirm or deny her infidelity, and the husband died without knowing the truth of the matter.

Hanged for Half-a-crown

In 1823, Britain's Secretary of Home Affairs, Sir Robert Peel, was instrumental in abolishing the death penalty for some hundred offences. Prior to the 1823 reforms, more than two hundred offences had been capital crimes, but for humanitarian reasons Peel had managed to reduce these by about half. However, this still left many trivial transgressions carrying the extreme penalty. Indeed, 18-year-old Londoner Joseph Harwood was hanged the following year for stealing half-a-crown (12½p), although the charge was called highway robbery under the country's antiquated criminal code. Harwood became the family breadwinner in his early teens following the death of his labourer father in an accident. The young man became a self-employed street trader and soon earned a lucrative living, bringing in as much as ten shillings a day, a very good wage at that time. But his mother had difficulty controlling him, and Harwood fell into bad company, often drinking and womanising for days on end. In fact, he later admitted that his financial success had contributed to his eventual downfall, saying that he would never have got into trouble had he earned less money and worked for an employer.

Harwood's luck ran out after he witnessed a tiff in a public house between a woman and a drunken Irishman. The drunk treated his female aquaintance to some liquor but then promptly refused to pay for it. So the woman removed his hat and gave it to the publican as a pledge. The Irishman's response was to strike the woman a violent blow, a gesture which led to a brawl involving several people. Later, after the incident had blown over, Harwood noticed the inebriated reveller sitting in a pub booth with his waistcoat undone. On the pretext of helping the man button up his garment, Harwood took the opportunity of filching half-a-crown from his pocket.

The drunk claimed that Harwood had beaten and robbed him, and accused him of being a member of a gang of thieves. Unfortunately for Harwood, who strongly denied complicity in any assault, the jury believed the complainant's story, and the youth was sentenced to death.

Shortly before Harwood's conviction Sheriff Sir Peter Laurie had decided that a further refinement was needed to improve the method of hanging at Newgate (Annual Register, 1824). He disliked the ritual of adjusting the rope to the proper length after it had been put around the sufferer's neck, thinking the operation both too lengthy and distressing to the condemned. A more humane technique was then in use at Glasgow but Laurie found it 'far too complicated to be entrusted to the Old Bailey executioners'. Instead, he came up with an idea of his own which proved acceptable to his brother Sheriff and the Gaol Committee. It was described as follows: 'From the beam is suspended a chain of hoops or circular links, which are covered with leather to prevent any clanking noise. The chain is nearly two feet in length. The rope is fixed to a hook, and by it attached instantly to any of the links of the chain, as the height of the culprit may require. As the statures of the culprits are known, the rope is adjusted by the hook on the chain, to the requisite length, and all is ready before the man is brought from the condemned cell.'

Laurie added that the operation took very little time, and also spared the feeling of the spectators by reducing the often prolonged agonies of the sufferers. His innovation seems to have been effective, for at the subsequent Harwood execution in May, the condemned man was 'but slightly convulsed' after the drop fell.

Attempt to Cheat the Gallows

Greed was the motive which inspired prosperous London bookseller Thomas Charles White, 23, to try and burn down his shop in order to claim the insurance. Had his crime, committed one night in August 1826, been successful, then it might have caused the deaths of several people who lodged above the premises in High Holborn. But luckily the plan went wrong, and the fire was quickly discovered and dealt with without casualty. White, a married man, was eventually tried and hanged the following January, although he had blamed a young woman servant for his own wicked deed.

It was events following his conviction, however, that produced the drama in this case. White's friends smuggled into him some fine spring saws to tackle the bars in his cell window, and with remarkable resourcefulness he used strong sewing thread to construct a makeshift but serviceable rope ladder so that he might scale the prison walls. However, the equipment was discovered before he could make his escape bid. Realising that the game was up, White told his captors that he would nevertheless elude them by committing suicide, so he was placed under constant guard.

But White had yet more tricks, as was witnessed by the mob at his execution. An onlooker recalled that on being prepared for death by the hangman, White somehow managed to free his pinioned arms and promptly pulled off the death cap which had covered his head and face. After being further secured, and just as the platform was about to fall from beneath him, White made a further violent effort and leaped forward to gain a foothold on the stationary plank. An observer recorded what happened next: 'His arms were again at liberty, and he instantly clung with both hands to the rope above his head, and thus he remained in an oblique position until he was pulled down by mere force. White, have resolutely refused to have the cap replaced on his head, exhibited an appalling spectacle during his convulsive struggles, but fortunately the noose fixed in its proper place, so that it did not appear that his perverse obstinacy caused the culprit's agony to be protracted.'

White's companion on the gallows was 30-year-old needlewoman Amelia Roberts, who had stolen goods worth £400 from her employer. She was arrested whilst fleeing England for Ireland where she intended to wed her lover. Witnesses claimed she showed calm courage on the scaffold despite White's desperate efforts to escape the hangman.

A Crime of Passion

Although last-minute rescues and reprieves may abound in fiction, such cliff-hanging good fortune is seldom a feature of real-life situations. In the sad case of James Abbott, a 28-year-old London glove maker, who stabbed his wife in a frenzy of sexual jealousy, there was to be no pardon, and this despite an expectation among the town's citizens of his certain deliverance from the noose. Indeed, on the day prior to his execution in 1828, Britain's Home Secretary Sir Robert Peel spent an anxious three hours considering a reprieve before finally deciding that the poor wretch should hang.

At his trial, Abbott's wife Hannah revealed that her spouse had attacked her with a knife in a fit of unreasoned jealousy whilst she was preparing for bed. She received serious wounds to her neck and throat before fleeing her home, bleeding badly, and leaving her three small children behind. She went to friends who rushed her to hospital where she remained for five weeks. She told the court that she had been married for nearly eight years, and that her husband 'was rather weak in his mind'. But despite her appalling injuries, she pleaded with the judge to spare her man's life. In mitigation, some neighbours also confirmed that Abbott was a man much troubled by jealousy, but he was nevertheless convicted of attempted murder and condemned to death.

Many of the spectators on the cold winter morning that Abbott met his end thought that his life would be spared right up to the moment that the rope was placed about his neck. But he died, together with small-time burglars John James and Joseph Mahoney, and gentleman-forger Joseph Hunton, a prominent London Quaker.

Hunton, aged 58, a part-owner of a warehouse in London's Ironmonger Lane, was convicted of passing a forged Bill of Exchange in the sum of £162. But he was also strongly suspected of passing other forgeries totalling some £5000. Realising that the game was up, Hunton abandoned his family and fled London, but he was captured by police aboard the vessel *Leeds* as it was about the leave St Helens for America.

Sadistic Mistresses

An appalling case of child cruelty, which ended in the death of 10-year-old Frances Colpit in East London, aroused much angry public interest in the spring of 1829. It was startlingly reminiscent of two cases of sadism which had occurred some sixty years earlier in the area – the harsh and heartless crimes of Elizabeth Brownrigg, and of a mother and daughter both named Sarah Metyard.

In the autumn of 1767, Elizabeth Brownrigg, a midwife employed at St Dunstan's workhouse, had been convicted of murdering her 17-year-old servant Mary Clifford. Brownrigg lived at Fleur de Lys Court, Fetter Lane, and kept sixteen teenage servant girls she had obtained from the nearby foundling hospital. She treated them very badly and frequently beat them at the slightest excuse. But she went too far in the case of Mary Clifford and a 13-year-old girl whom she imprisoned in the cellar for more than a year, where they worked at grinding colours for their master, a painter. The girls shared their terrible abode with a pig, and drank and fed from its trough. They ate only bread and water, and slept on the floor. The pair were often stripped naked, tied to a water pipe and flogged with canes, brooms and horse whips until they bled. Mary Clifford suffered so badly that she was eventually unable to speak, her head swelled to an enormous size, and she died.

A True representation of the Horrid Cruelty's Committed
y ELIZ.ᵗ BROWNRIGG on the Body of MARY CLIFFORD her Apprentic
31 of July 1767. for which the Aforesaid Eliz.ᵗʰ Brownrigg was Executed at Tyburn Sep.ᵗʰ 14

Elizabeth Brownrigg awaiting execution.

The case came to light after neighbours heard the girls' screams from the cellar and they notified the authorities. Brownrigg was tried for murder, along with her husband and son who were both jailed for less than a year, and throughout she showed no signs of repentance. She was jeered at all the way to her execution at Tyburn, and her body was given to the anatomists.

About a year later the awful crimes of the Metyards were revealed after being hidden for some years. Mrs Metyard was a milliner who shared her home in Bruton Street with her daughter and five orphan girls she had acquired from foundling hospitals. Among them was an ailing youngster called Anne Naylor and her sister. As in the Brownrigg case, all the girls were subjected to ill-treatment. Half-starved and often beaten, Anne fled twice but was caught and punished by Mrs Metyard and her violent daughter. Following a particularly severe battering, the child was tied and secured in the standing position so that she could not sit down, and was deprived of food. The unfortunate girl died three days later from exhaustion.

Anne's sister became the next victim of the vicious women, and was strangled after showing concern at Anne's disappearance. Both bodies were then dismembered and disposed of.

And there the matter rested for a decade. But 'murder will out', as the old adage goes, and so it proved in this instance. Enraged at her daughter eloping with a lodger called Mr Rooker, the irate mother tracked the pair down to Ealing, West London. The two women then had a row in the presence of Rooker and the murders were mentioned. The perturbed Mr Rooker duly confided his fears to the proper authority, and both Metyards were quickly tried, convicted and deservedly hanged for murder.

The Frances Colpit affair started in April 1828, when the girl was transferred from St Martin's parish workhouse to join six other resident child apprentices at the home of Mrs Esther Hibner in nearby Platt Terrace, East London. Hibner, 61, who was assisted by her daughter, also named Esther, and their forewoman Ann Robinson, had agreed to feed and house the youngsters, as well as teach them the trade of tambour worker. But the children, who had been in good health on arrival at the Hibner house, were used as mere slave labour. They were ill-treated, badly-clothed, and fed on a starvation diet. Relatives of the apprentices, who were seldom allowed to see the children, became suspicious of the neglect and reported their fears to workhouse officials.

When parish overseer John Blackman investigated, a catalogue of horrors was revealed. He said he found all the children in a most wretched state, and a surgeon who accompanied Blackman on his visit was particularly shocked at the condition of young Frances Colpit. He reported that 'She seemed merely skin and bone. She was

113

dreadfully emaciated, her lips were contracted, and there was a redness about her eyes. And she had bruises on her arms and forehead.' The unfortunate girl, together with the other children, was immediately taken to the St Pancras infirmary where, despite dedicated medical care, she died a month later. Surgeon Benjamin Bury gave the cause of death as consumption, brought on by lack of food.

Hibner, her daughter and Ann Robinson were arrested and jointly charged with the wilful murder of the child.

Former apprentice Susan Whitby, who had worked alongside Frances, revealed some of the hellish treatment she and others had been forced to endure. 'She [Francis Colpit] used to have a slice of bread and a cup of milk and water at breakfast time; she had nothing else in the course of the day, and not other meal until the next morning ... she had her breakfast at half-past eight o'clock, and was allowed five minutes to eat it in. Sometimes they used to say that she had not earned her breakfast, and should not have it, and they would giver her potatoes at one o'clock. When she had potatoes for dinner she had nothing else all day. Once a fortnight, on Sundays, we all had meat.'

Susan said that her mistress had kept a dog, and that she had seen Frances and other hungry apprentices eat bits of fish and meat they took from the animal's food. She also claimed that the three women had regularly flogged Frances with a rod, cane and slipper, and she once saw Hibner's daughter take up the girl by the heels and dip her head into a bucket of dirty water.

The three accused denied the charge. Hibner senior, however, was convicted and sentenced to death, but the others were acquitted. A man who attended the trial recorded later that Hibner was perfectly unmoved when the sentence of death was pronounced, and on her removal from the dock exclaimed, in a loud and distinct voice: 'Well, they have done their best; but though they have given me the law, they have not given me justice.'

On the Sunday before her execution, Hibner tried to commit suicide by stabbing herself in the neck, but she was caught in the act and prevented from killing herself. She then went into a violent frenzy and had to be put into a straitjacket.

Hibner refused to receive any religious consolation, and declined the Reverend Dr Cotton's request to attend her on the scaffold. She was hanged before the largest crowd assembled at a Newgate execution since the 100,000-strong mob gathered there for the death of the gentleman-forger Henry Fauntleroy, some four years earlier.

A Touch of Larceny

There was an air of comic about the crime committed in the early summer of 1831 by one George Widgett, for the culprit, who stole 52 sheep which had been left to graze in the then rural area of Lewisham, subsequently kept them just around the corner from London's Worship Street police station.

The police naturally soon showed a professional interest in their new four-legged neighbours, and official inquiries quickly resolved the puzzle. But Widgett, the father of several children, not surprisingly did not see the funny side of the matter when he was convicted of the capital offence of theft and sentenced to death. He died in tears alongside opportunistic thief John Broach.

Broach's modus operandi was to obtain employment as a servant in the London homes of prosperous people whom he then robbed. He generally filched items of plate, jewellery and furniture, which he then pawned, but by the very nature of his thefts, it was only a matter of time before he was inevitably caught, tried and condemned.

He was survived by a wife and child.

The Body-snatchers

For most people, the term 'body-snatchers' will instantly evoke the names of William Burke and William Hare, the two Irish fiends whose gruesome exploits have forever gained them a leading place in the annals of infamy. In fact, they never were grave robbers, but instead suffocated their victims and sold the bodies to unscrupulous medical men, a practice which soon acquired the notorious title of 'burking'.

But what about the ghouls who prowled London in search of bodies, and those who also murdered to obtain corpses for sale to anatomists during the early years of the last century? One man, John Bishop, spent a busy twelve years stealing an estimated 1000 bodies, and he murdered at least three people.

According to The Newgate Calendar, body-snatching was already a thriving business by the middle of the eighteenth century. It was a vile trade which flourished because of an inconsistency in the law. The government demanded high standards from surgeons, yet it would not change its laws to allow an adequate supply of bodies for

115

medical research, and for operations to be carried out correctly on the living it was essential to have properly trained surgeons. This meant that anatomy schools were only too ready to buy a steady supply of bodies, and the staff did not bother to inquire too carefully as to their origin. There thus existed a busy trade in the dead. Their activities are described by the Calendar:

> These impious robbers are vulgarly termed resurrection men, but should rather be called sacrilegious robbers of our holy Church, not even confining the unnatural crime to men alone, for the gentler sex are connected in this horrid traffic, whose business it is to strip off the shroud, or whatever garments in which the body may have been wrapped, and to sell them, while the men, through the darkness of the night, drag the naked bodies to be anatomized.
>
> Though it matters little where we return to our original dust, yet there is something offensive to the living to hear of graves being violated for this base purpose; and to know that the remains of a parent, a wife, or a child, have been thus removed, is shocking to our nature.
>
> When Hunter, the famous anatomist, was in full practice, he had a surgical theatre behind his house in Windmill Street, where he gave lectures to a very numerous class of pupils. To this place such numbers of dead bodies were brought, during the winter season, that the mob rose several times, and were upon the point of pulling down his house. He had a well dug in the back part of his premises, in which was thrown the putrid flesh, and with it alkalis, in order to hasten its consumption.
>
> Numberless are the instances of dead bodies being seized on their way to the surgeons. Hackney coachmen, for an extra fare, and porters with hampers, are often employed by these resurrection men for this purpose.

Quoting from a monthly publication of March 1776, the report added:

> The remains of more than twenty dead bodies were discovered in a shed in Tottenham Court Road, supposed to have been deposited there by traders to the surgeons; of whom there is one, it is said, in the Borough, who makes an open profession of dealing in dead bodies, and is well known by the name of the Resurrectionist.

"The Resurrectionists" by Thomas Rowlandson

Still more shocking is it to be told that men who are paid for protecting the sacred deposit of the mortal remains of their fellow-parishioners are often confederates, as the present case will demonstrate.

It then went on to tell of Bloomsbury gravedigger Peter Williams and his assistant John Holmes, who together with their accomplice Esther Donaldson removed the body of Mrs Jane Sainsbury from the St George's Church graveyard. But they were caught red-handed before they could sell the body, which was identified by the distraught widower. Tried at the Sessions House in December 1777, the woman was unaccountably acquitted, but Williams and Holmes were each sentenced to six months' imprisonment. They were also severely whipped through crowds of approving spectators along a half-mile route between Holborn and St Giles.

A variation on body-snatching was the cheeky theft of a lead coffin from the Aldermanbury Church vault, resulting in the appearance of three men in court in April 1778. The crime was revealed by James Gould, who gave King's Evidence against his fellow-thieves George Roach and Robert Elliot, and scrap metal dealer Jonas Parker. He said that he, Roach and Elliot, who were journeymen carpenters, stole the leaden interior of a coffin while working at the church, but they were caught selling the cut-up pieces of lead to Parker.

The lead was identified as coming from a Mr Thornton's coffin after the nameplate was found in Roach's home. Although Parker claimed he did not know that the lead had been stolen, it was well known that people in his trade could easily recognise coffin lead, and he was convicted of receiving. Roach, Elliot and Parker were sentenced to three years' hard labour.

A tragic element in the case of body-snatcher Elizabeth Ross, who murdered 84-year-old street hawker Caroline Walsh, is that the killer was convicted on the evidence of her schoolboy son. Although Ross, 38, was hanged for her crime, it is hardly conceivable that her common-law-husband Cook, who was also a well-known London body-snatcher, was not implicated in the killing, for he was in the room of their Whitechapel home whilst the slaying took place. But their son, Edward Cook, aged 12, cleared his father of any involvement in the crime, saying that the man had sat looking out of the window during the murder and removal of the body, ignorant of what went on.

The victim, who made a living by selling laces and ribbons, was known to Ross, and she readily accepted her invitation to have a cup of coffee and a rest on the family bed. The story is taken up by young Edward, who said that after the hawker dozed off, his mother smothered her by clapping her hands on her mouth. The lad explained: 'She kept her hand on her mouth I dare say for half an hour, until the lady appeared to be dead. Some time after, my mother carried her body downstairs. She lifted it off the bed herself. She carried it like a loose baby in her arms.' Next day, the boy found a sack in a corner of the cellar, containing the old woman's corpse. But the body soon disappeared, and there can be no doubt that Ross had sold it to surgeons.

The killing came to light after the old lady was missed by friends, and inquiries revealed that Ross had sold the deceased's clothes to a second-hand dealer.

During her trial in 1832, Ross claimed that her son's evidence was false throughout, and she never admitted her guilt. On her way to execution (and subsequent dissection), the killer reportedly said: 'Oh my child, my deluded child, thus to hang her who suffered for you!'

In the summer of 1831, shortly before he was to become involved in the infamous 'Italian Boy' murder case, body-snatcher Thomas Williams, aged 26, was charged with breaking into a house in Hackney Road, East London, and stealing the corpse of a widow's teenage son. A brief report in *The Times* tells us:

> The poor woman had left her home for a short time only, and on her return found the corpse had, in the meantime, been stolen. Some of the female neighbours then recollected ... a man passed them with a basket containing something which smelt very offensively, and occasioned them to look particularly at the man, although they had no suspicion, until the alarm was given, that he was carrying off the corpse of the widow's son. A pursuit was immediately commenced, but without success. From the description given, however, a policeman apprehended Williams on the

A newly-buried body dug up by the body-snatchers Peter Williams and John Holmes and accomplices, to be sold to the anatomists.

following morning, and he was identified by the females as the man whom they had seen near the house with a basket as stated. No trace of the body, nor of the manner in which it had been disposed of, could be discovered, nor any further evidence obtained, and, after an examination before a magistrate, the prisoner was discharged upon a recognizance.

An astonishing account of premature burial, an encounter with body-snatchers, and a last-minute escape from the surgeon's scalpel, was related by Scotsman John MacIntire, who was buried alive in Edinburgh in April 1824 whilst in a trance. I give the remarkable story in his own words:

> I had been some time ill of a slow and lingering fever. My strength gradually wasted and I could see by the doctor that I had nothing to hope. One day towards evening, I was seized with strange and incredible quivering. I saw around my bed innumerable strange faces; they were bright and visionary, and without bodies. There was light and solemnity, and I tried to move but could not. I could recollect with perfectness, but the power of motion had departed. I heard the sound of weeping at my pillow ... and the voice of the nurse say, 'He is dead.' I cannot describe at what I felt at those words. I exerted my utmost power to stir myself, but I could not move even an eyelid. My father drew his hand over my face, and closed my eyelids. The world was then darkened, but I could still hear, and feel and suffer.
>
> For three days a number of friends called to see me, I heard them in low accents speak of what I was; and more than one touched me with his finger. The coffin was then procured, and I was laid in it. I felt the coffin lifted and borne away. I heard and felt it placed in the hearse ... it halted, the coffin was taken out ... I felt myself carried on the shoulders of men, I heard the cords of the coffin moved, I felt it swing as dependent by them. It was lowered and rested upon the bottom of the grave.
>
> Dreadful was the effort I then made to exert the power of action, but my whole frame was immoveable. The sound of the rattling mould as it covered me, was far more tremendous than thunder. This also ceased and all was silent. This is death, thought I, and soon the worms will be crawling about my flesh. In the contemplation of this hideous thought, I heard a low sound in the earth over me, and I fancied that the worms and reptiles were coming. The sound continued to grow louder and nearer. Can it be possible, thought I, that my friends suspect they have buried me

too soon? The hope was truly like light bursting through the gloom of death. The sound ceased. They dragged me out of the coffin by the head, and carried me swiftly away. When borne to some distance I was thrown down like a clod, and by the interchange of one or two brief sentences, I discovered that I was in the hands of two of those robbers, who live by plundering the grave, and selling the bodies of parents, and children, and friends.

Being rudely stripped of my shroud, I was placed naked on a table. In a short time I heard by the bustle in the room, that the doctors and students were assembling. When all was ready the demonstrator took his knife, and pierced my bosom. I felt a dreadful crackling, as it were, through my whole frame, a convulsive shudder instantly followed, and a shriek of horror rose from all present. The ice of death was broken up ... my trance was ended! The utmost exertions were made to restore me, and in the course of an hour I was in full possession of all my faculties.

One shudders to think what might have happened had the body-snatchers realised that MacIntire was still alive.

Why did 33-year-old John Bishop, a married man with three children, in a time of widespread poverty and unemployment, decide to kill for bodies instead of continuing with his long-established and comparatively safe, lucrative trade as a resurrection man?

There is no doubt that he became brutalized during his years as a body-snatcher, for he often boasted of his exploits to anyone who cared to listen to him at his local tavern, until the landlord and patrons showed such dislike of his company that he decided to drink eslewhere.

The new place he chose was 'The Fortune of War', a haunt of body-snatchers in Giltspur Street near Newgate Prison. It was there that he met 33-year-old fellow-resurrectionist James May, with whom he became very friendly. Bishop particularly admired the way that May, who was so devoted to his 'trade', had taken up lodgings in a house bordering a workhouse graveyard, where he had an ample supply of bodies which would not be missed by caring relatives.

Bishop also befriended bricklayer Thomas Williams (whom we have already met), who was fascinated by Bishop's tales of the dangers of his profession. When Bishop invited him to become a partner in crime, he readily agreed, but upon condition that they forget body-snatching and become 'burkers' instead.

Despite bungling two early attempts at their new calling, the trio soon perfected a technique of drugging their victims prior to drowning them in a well in Bishop's back garden.

Their first admitted murder was that of 35-year-old Fanny Pigburn, a cabinet maker's widow described as being 'thin, rather tall, and very much marked with the smallpox'. Bishop said they had met her late one October night after she had been evicted by her landlord. They found her sitting on a doorstep in Shoreditch with her five-year-old child on her lap. The body-snatchers took her to Bishop's home in Bethnal Green where she spent the night. She left very early the next morning after arranging to see the men again that lunchtime.

The trio kept their rendezvous at a pub called 'The London Apprentice', where the men bought Fanny drinks and gave her some money. She said she had left the child with a friend. On parting, they arranged a further meeting for later that evening. That night, they had a few drinks together before the men took Fanny to an empty house near Bishop's home, where they drugged and killed her.

Next day, the murderers, accompanied by a friend named Shields, sold their victim's body for eight guineas to James Appleton, the procurator at the quaintly-named Mr Grainger's Anatomical Theatre in Webb Street, Southwark.

A fortnight later, Bishop and Williams killed an 11-year-old boy called Cunningham, who had lived rough on the London streets after running away from home a year earlier. The killers found the youngster asleep in the pig market at Smithfield. They dealt with him in the same fashion as they had Fanny Pigburn, before selling his body to a medical school without arousing suspicion.

Although their gruesome and cold-blooded crimes had gone undetected, Bishop and Williams made a fatal error when they despatched their final victim – the Italian boy!

The lad, Carlo Ferrier, was brought to England from Italy in July 1830, at the age of 14, to work for a street organ player. But after a few weeks he left his employer and made a living doing odd jobs and begging. He often stood in London's Haymarket and Oxford Street with a revolving cage containing two white mice hanging round his neck.

The story of the cruel murder of Carlo on the evening of 3 November 1831, after the boy had been lured to Bishop's house on the pretext of giving him work, was given in Bishop's eve-of-execution confession, from which I give the following extract:

We [Bishop and Williams] lighted a candle and gave the boy some bread and cheese, and after he had eaten, we gave him a cup full of rum, with about half a small phial of laudanum in it. The boy drank it in two draughts and afterwards a little beer. In about ten minutes he fell asleep on the chair in which he sat, and I removed him from the chair to the floor, and laid him on his side. We then went out and left him there.

We had a quartern of gin and a pint of beer at 'The Feathers', near Shoreditch Church, and then went home again, having been away from the boy for about twenty minutes. We found him asleep as we had left him. We took him directly, asleep and insensible, into the garden, and tied a cord to his feet to enable us to pull him up by, and I then took him in my arms and let him slide from them headlong into the well in the garden, whilst Williams held the cord to prevent the body going altogether too low in the well. He was nearly wholly in the water of the well ... his feet just above the surface. Williams fastened the other end of the cord round the paling, to prevent the body getting beyond our reach. The boy struggled a little with his arms and legs in the water, and the water bubbled for a minute. We waited till these symptoms were past, and then went indoors, and afterwards I think we went out and walked down Shoreditch to occupy the time, and in about three quarters of an hour we returned and took him out of the well by pulling up by the cord attached to his feet. We undressed him in the paved yard, rolled his clothes up and buried them. We carried the boy into the wash-house, laid him on the floor, and covered him with a bag.

Shortly before noon the next day, Bishop and May turned up at the dissecting rooms at London's King's College, where they told the porter, William Hill, that they had a 'fresh subject' for sale. But Hill did not seem interested in the body of a 14-year-old boy, so, although they had not brought the corpse with them, Bishop and May haggled with anatomy demonstrator Richard Partridge over a

The Italian boy, murdered for his body. His teeth were sold to a dentist.

price. Finally, Bishop agreed to return with the body that afternoon and sell it for nine guineas, although May, who was drunk, demanded ten guineas.

The body was duly delivered by Bishop and May, who were this time accompanied by Williams and Shields. On examining the corpse, which had a swollen face, bloodshot eyes, a strange rigidity of the limbs and a cut over the left temple, Partridge was immediately suspicious about the cause of death. On asking about this, he was told that it was none of his business. Partridge decided to contact the police, and stalled the 'burkers' by agreeing to buy the body. Saying that he had only a £50 note, he left to get change, but instead returned with the police and the four men were arrested.

The next day, Carlo's body was thoroughly examined by Partridge and a team of doctors, who agreed that death had been caused by violence. They also found that twelve teeth had been extracted from the jaw, and it was later proved that May had sold them to a dentist for a shilling each.

Shields was soon cleared of any part in the crime, but evidence of the guilt of the others quickly came to light. Police inquiries led to the identification of Carlo, and some of Bishop's neighbours recalled seeing the lad in their street shortly before his death. Bishop's next-door neighbour, William Woodcock, told how he had been awakened during the early hours of one morning by the sound of three men's footsteps in Bishop's house, followed by the scuffle which had lasted for a minute or two. He had also heard voices, one of which he recognised as that of Williams. A search of Bishop's house revealed bloodstained tools, chisels, a file and a bradawl, which had been used to extract the teeth, as well as clothing found buried in the garden. To complete the damning picture, a boy who lived nearby said he had seen Bishop's children playing with two white mice.

The killers denied their guilt throughout their trial. Bishop claimed he had stolen the body from a grave, but would not reveal the location of the graveyard because he did not want to implicate the watchman there. Williams and May said that they had merely helped dispose of the body without knowing where it had come from, but on the eve of their execution, Bishop and Williams finally confessed, and they cleared May of any involvement in the brutal murder.

May, described as a 'tall, light-haired and rather good-looking man', went into a state of total collapse when Newgate Ordinary, the Rev. Dr Cotton, told him of his last-minute reprieve. A most graphic account of this emotional moment was penned by a reporter for *The Times*, who wrote:

No sooner had Dr Cotton repeated the words, 'That the execution of the sentence upon John May shall be respited during His Majesty's gracious pleasure,' than the poor wretch fell to the earth as if struck by lightning. His arms worked with the most frightful contortions, and four of the officers of the prison could with difficulty hold him; his countenance assumed a livid paleness ... the blood forsook his lips ... his eyes appeared set, and pulsation at the heart could not be distinguished. All persons present thought that he could not possibly survive. ... it was believed, indeed, that the warrent of mercy had proved his death blow.

Mr Wontner [prison governor] and Dr Cotton, who have of course witnessed many scenes of dreadful agitation during their experience among capital convicts, declare that they never before beheld any human being so fearfully affected.

It was nearly a quarter of an hour before May was restored to the use of his faculties. At last, when recollection returned, he attempted to clasp his hands in the attitude of thanksgiving, but his limbs shook so violently that he found even that was impossible. His lips moved, but nothing but inarticulate sounds came from his tongue. The parties present soothed him with assurance that they knew what he meant to say, and with earnest entreaties that he would calm himself, and not attempt to speak. When restored to something like composure, May poured forth his gratitude to God, and his thanks to the humane gentlemen who had interested themselves in his behalf.

He then explained that when Dr Cotton commenced reading the warrant he thought that all hope was at an end ... that the ceremony was to signify to him that he must die ... the sudden revulsion of feeling when he heard the words we have quoted, caused him to swoon. He added, that on learning he was to be spared, he felt as if his heart had burst in his bosom ... he hoped now to lead a better life, and to evince his gratitude to God by sincere repentance.

But he never recovered from the shock, and it led to his premature death a few weeks later. His demise was briefly recorded by a few lines in *The Times*, 23 January 1832, 'Death of May, the Alleged Burkite. May, the convict, who was tried at the Old Bailey, with Bishop and Williams, and sentenced to death, which sentence was afterwards commuted to transportation for life, died on Friday morning. The shock produced upon his mind by the unexpected communication of his reprieve is stated to have been the cause of his illness, which was considerably augmented by the intolerable annoy-

127

ances which he experienced from the convicts on board of the hulks. He was removed from several convict ships, but he sunk under his sufferings on board the ship *Grampus*.'

Bishop and Williams met their just end on a cold December morning in 1831 before a crowd of some 40,000 people, and many spectators were injured in the crush. Bishop died almost immediately, but Williams died hard, struggling on the rope for several minutes. The two bodies were later transferred to different medical schools for dissection, Bishop's ending up at King's College ... the very place where he had tried to sell the body of the Italian boy.

The old adage, that some good may result from evil, certainly proved true in this instance, for the case led to parliamentary reforms the following year which effectively stopped the body-snatching trade.

The Edgware Road Murder

What became known as the Edgware Road murder stirred the nation's popular imagination during the early weeks of 1837, for the discovery in various parts of London of the pieces of a woman's dismembered body was a very unusual event in the criminal annals of the early years of the last century. In those day, murders were mainly spur-of-the-moment killings committed during robberies, rather than being well-planned, cold-blooded crimes.

The horrific event first came to light on 28 December 1836, when the trunk of the victim's body was found wrapped in a sack near the Pineapple toll bar, Edgware Road. A few days later, on 6 January, the head was found at Stepney in Johnson's Lock, in the Regents Canal and the legs and thighs were discovered a month later in a sack dumped among bushes in an osier bed in Coldharbour Lane, between Camberwell and Brixton.

The killer of Hannah Brown, James Greenacre, seems to have been a resourceful rogue from his early days. At the tender age of 13, with £20 in his pocket (he had persuaded his parents he needed the cash for his apprenticeship fees) he left his native Norfolk for London. Finding it hard to get work, it is said he resorted to subterfuge to jump the jobless queue, and bribed an official at *The Times* newspaper to show him copies of vacancies advertisements before they appeared in print, a claim which was later rejected by a newspaper spokesman as being 'too ridiculous to need refutation'. Whatever the truth of the matter, Greenacre soon got a job in a grocery shop near Tower Hill, where he stayed for three years, and managed to save £45.

By the age of 21 he had acquired his own grocery business in Woolwich, which he later transferred to Southwark. But after having trouble with the excise laws he fled to New York, where he spent some two trouble-filled years. On hearing of the death of his third wife in London, he remarried in America, but eventually returned to Britain alone, to reside at 6 Carpenter's Place, Camberwell, where he made peppermint rock and invented a patent washing machine.

Greenacre had two children by each of his first three wives. When he met Hannah Brown some time in 1836, he had already acquired a 35-year-old mistress, Sarah Gale, who lived with him at Camberwell. But this did not deter Greenacre from proposing marriage to his future victim, a former housekeeper with ambitions to own a fruit and pastry shop, although she had been reduced to making a living as a washerwoman. Despite Hannah Brown's poor circumstances, Greenacre appeared to think she owned some property, and he arranged their wedding for Christmas Day 1836. Perhaps he was taken in by her 'fine, genteel, sober and respectable appearance', qualities ascribed to her by a neighbour, who also described her as having 'very long brown hair, fair complexion, high forehead and longish features, with very good teeth.'

Announcing his wedding plans to friends, he said that he and his new wife would soon live in Hudson's Bay, Canada, where he had a great deal of property. Poor Hannah Brown, at Greenacre's insistence, sold her possessions and furniture in early December, and on the Christmas Eve afternoon he helped her move house, taking with them her remaining things in a hackney coach.

Hannah's friend, Mrs Catherine Glass, said she last saw her on Christmas Eve, when she had seemed perfectly happy and well, and was looking forward to her marriage the next day at St Giles Church. But one of Hannah's neighbours, a Mrs Davis, was surprised to receive a visit from Greenacre on Christmas Eve, who told her he had called off the wedding because he had discovered that his wife-to-be did not possess the property that she had claimed to own.

Hannah Brown's murder was surely premeditated, for on December 22, Sarah Gale rented the back parlour of a Mr Henry Wignal's house at 56 Portland Street, Walworth, where Mr Wignal first met Greenacre the following day, and where Greenacre dined with Gale on Christmas Day.

In fact, Greenacre and Gale moved out of their Camberwell address a week after Christmas, hiring help to move their sealed boxes and furniture.

By early January, Hannah Brown's head was preserved in spirits at the Paddington poorhouse, where it was later identified, and Greenacre was quickly tracked down and charged with murder. Whilst admitting responsibility for the poor woman's death, Greenacre claimed it had been 'a very melancholy and unfortunate accident as ever befell man.'

He told the court that on Christmas Eve Hannah Brown had drunk heavily during the morning and had insisted on having a great deal of rum in the evening. Greenacre had thought it an appropriate time to ask her about her financial situation. He explained:

> I told her that she had often dropped insinuations in my hearing about having property to go into business and she had said that she could command £300 or £400 at any time. I said that I had made some inquiry relative to her character, and had ascertained that she had been to Mr Smith's in Long Acre, a tally shop, to endeavour to procure silk gowns in my name.
>
> When I put these questions to her, she put on a feigned laugh, and retaliated by saying she thought I was deceiving her by mis-representing the extent of my own property.
>
> During this conversation she was reeling backwards and for-wards in her chair, which was on the swing. And, as I am deter-mined to adhere strictly to the truth, I must say that I put my foot to the chair. It was just after we had concluded tea, and she went back with a great violence against a chump of wood that I had been using of (sic), and that alarmed me very much. I went round the table and took her by the hand and kept shaking her, and she appeared entirely gone.
>
> As it regarded my own feelings, it is impossible to give any-thing like a description from the agitation I was in at the time. During this state of excitement, I deliberated and came to the determination of concealing her death in the manner in which it has already been laid before the world.

However, a surgeon testified that the victim had been killed by a blow to the front of the head, causing a corresponding bruise at the back of the head. Greenacre had then cut up the body, put the parts into sacks, and deposited them in various places around London.

In a prison suicide attempt, Greenacre was found lying on his back with a silk handkerchief tied to a noose around his right foot, and the other part of the handkerchief tied round his neck. He was unconscious when discovered in his cell. On being resuscitated he said: 'I don't thank you for what you have done. Damn the man who is afraid to die ... I am not!'

Although he showed little fear of death, Greenacre was more than reluctant to face the mob of 20,000 people which bayed for his blood at his inevitable execution outside Newgate Prison in late March. In fact, the ladykiller begged officials for a speedy death, pleading: 'Don't leave me long in the concourse.' His wish was granted, for an eyewitness said later that he had never seen an execution so quickly performed.

And what of Greenacre's mistress, Sarah Gale? She was transported to Australia for life after being convicted of complicity to murder.

The Courvoisier case

There was only one execution at Newgate in the year 1840, but it was an event that attracted a crowd of about 20,000 onlookers, including Charles Dickens and William Makepeace Thackeray, and the actor Charles Kean. For the mob was fascinated by the gory crime which had led 23-year-old Francois Benjamin Courvoisier, a Swiss valet, to the scaffold.

In fact, many witnesses to the July hanging paid high fees for the privilege of obtaining places at strategic windows which afforded a good view of the proceedings. Some others even risked life and limb by perching precariously on the roofs of nearby houses to watch the death of the servant who had brutally killed his 73-year-old master, Lord William Russell, at his Park Lane home.

In an eve-of-execution confession, Courvoisier revealed that he had turned to crime after becoming disillusioned with his job. He initially planned to rob his rich master of £30 or £40, but then it occurred to him that he might hide the theft by murdering his employer and faking a robbery. He accordingly laid careful plans, but for a while his conscience troubled him and he failed to act. However, on the evening of 5 May, 1840, following a disagreement with Lord Russell, the valet fulfilled his evil intentions. Describing the cruel killing, Courvoisier wrote:

> 'While he was in bed I went down to the kitchen, where I remained about an hour and a half. During that time I placed all the things in the state in which they were [found] in the morning. I went upstairs, and going by the dining room I entered into it and took out a carving knife. I went up to my master's bedroom. When I opened the door I heard him asleep, and stopped for a while thinking of what I was about to do; but the evil disposition of my heart did not allow me to repent. I turned up my coat and shirt sleeves and came near to the bed where a rushlight was burning. I hardened myself to my conscience and threw myself upon my victim and murdered him with the knife I was holding in my hand. I then wiped my hand and knife with a towel which I placed on Lord William's body.'

Indeed, Courvoisier's attack was so violent that the victim's head was almost severed from the body, but it was carried out so quickly and silently that it did not even disturb the cook, Mary Hannell, and housemaid, Sarah Manser, who occupied the chamber immediately above their master's bedroom. The killer then searched the room for money, and finding much more cash than he had anticipated, he hid some of it about the house. Finally, after returning downstairs and quietly fabricating a break-in, he calmly went to bed and fell into a peaceful sleep.

He was aroused early the next morning by the frantic housemaid who had found her master's writing room apparently ransacked. Courvoisier rushed downstairs and, feigning dismay, said:' Some person has been robbing; for God's sake go and see where his lordship is!' When questioned later by police, Courvoisier is claimed to have fallen back into a chair and said: 'This is a shocking job. I shall lose my place, and lose my character.'

But the police quickly suspected Courvoisier after finding cash and jewellery hidden behind the skirting board in the butler's pantry.

Courvoisier's case marked the end of a long Newgate tradition — that of the preaching of the condemned sermon. He was the last killer to endure this ordeal, and it was an event which attracted many members of the public, including some members of the nobility, a

Opposite: Courvoisier's death mask.

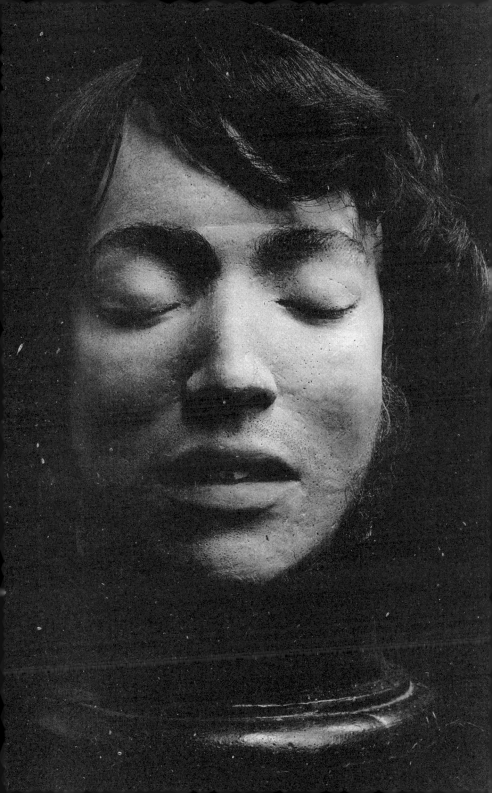

few ladies, and several members of the House of Commons. Contemporary accounts give a minute description of the demeanour of the convict on that solemn occasion. He sat on a bench before the pulpit (the condemned pew had been removed) and never once raised his eyes during the service. 'In fact,' an onlooker recorded, 'his looks denoted extreme sorrow and contrition, and he seemed to suffer great inward agitation when the Ordinary particularly alluded to the crime for the perpetration of which he stood condemned. The Ordinary seems to have addressed himself directly to Courvoisier, and to have dwelt with more emphasis than good taste upon the nature of the crime, and the necessity for repentance. But the Chaplain admitted that the solitude of the convict's cell was more appropriate for serious reflection and profitable ministration than "this exciting occasion before a large and public assembly."'

There can be no doubt that as executions became more rare they made more impression on the public, but for the London throng which gathered to watch Courvoisier die, the event must have seemed somewhat of an anti-climax. They were perhaps disappointed by the murderer's calm and unmoved attitude during his final minutes, and they may have felt cheated as they saw the Swiss valet die quickly and easily in an attitude of prayer, his bound raised hands slowly sinking with the ebbing of his life.

Death on Battersea Bridge

Rightly or wrongly, it is a popular British belief that Continental people, particularly the French, possess an ardent nature. Many feel that the French law recognizes such a fiery quality in its citizens, and indeed shows a curious leniency towards those who prove that they commit their crimes in moments of passion. But British law shows no such sensitivity for its transgressors. So it was perhaps particularly unfortunate for Frenchman Auguste Dalmas, a prosperous 50-year-old chemist, that he killed his mistress in London during a fit of sexual jealousy. It was a desperate act which cost him his life.

The first hint of the terrible crime came as a Mr William Parkins was crossing Battersea Bridge at about 10 pm on 29 April, 1844. He said that he had heard a cry from across the bridge and saw the female victim approaching him, staggering as though drunk. It was only when they met and she clung to him saying, 'Someone has cut me,' that he saw she was covered in blood from a terrible wound in her throat. Parkins took her to the toll house, where she was laid on the ground as a crowd gathered. One onlooker identified the dying woman as Mrs Sara M'Farlane. Hearing this, someone else said, 'Then Dalmas has done it!'

The lady was soon moved to the bar of the nearby Swan Tavern where she died some five minutes later, but she survived long enough to answer questions put to her by policeman Frederick Langton. She appeared lucid to the end, and the constable asked the pub's landlord, Mr William Gosling, to pay careful attention to what Mrs M'Farlane said.

But the trial judge refused to hear their evidence, ruling it inadmissible.

Other witnesses confirmed that Dalmas and his mistress had been seen earlier on that fatal evening enjoying a drink and strolling the streets together. Some, however, claimed to have heard Dalmas speaking angrily to his partner. The couple were well-known in the area, but would nevertheless have been conspicuous in their fashionable attire. Dalmas was his usual impeccable self, adorned in a smart frock coat and trousers, and sporting his continental-style, broad-brimmed hat, while his companion was genteelly turned out in a straw Tuscan bonnet, light gown and a coloured shawl with a dark border.

Dalmas, a widower, had four daughters, and he was hoping to marry Mrs M'Farlane, aged 45, who although herself had a son and daughter, was unattached and, as one of her friends remarked, 'was her own mistress and could do as she liked.'

The Frenchman did not return to his Brompton home after his night out, and he was not seen again until some days later, when he gave himself up at Marylebone Police Station. He walked in and said: 'I wish to surrender myself to you. I am haunted to death by the reports in the newspapers; they are all wrong.'

Dalmas was convicted on purely circumstantial evidence, although he maintained his innocence to the end, and despite a thorough examination of his clothing, no bloodstains were found. The chemist admitted being with the victim prior to her attack, but he claimed that he had left her at the foot of Battersea Bridge, where she was close to home in Bridge Road, to avoid paying the toll fee.

Some letters were found among the dead woman's belongings, all written by Dalmas, and mostly bordering on the obscene. At his trial, his defence counsel said that the disgusting letters showed that

Dalmas had an affection for Mrs M'Farlane amounting almost to madness. Indeed, another letter indicates his tormented state of mind at the time, and surely points to his guilt. It is addressed to his daughters Caroline, Charlotte, Sophia and Augusta, and reads: 'To my unfortunate family – Be it known that infernal prostitute M'Farlane, that second Millwood, has brought me to perdition; she has robbed me and my family under the mask of affection; has led me into all sorts of debauchery; her profligate and illicit intercourse with that married man Meredith, the nephew of Breeze the linen draper of Kensington, at the very time she had offered to become my wife, has made me come to the determination of committing suicide. I have been adoring a common prostitute, who now insults me in the most revolting manner. To have been mad enough to put my affection on a swearing, cursing, blaspheming, gin-drinking washerwoman and a whore, has turned my brain; I can live no longer; let the world know her, and may this prevent other victims from falling into her infernal snares. A. Dalmas.'

Dalmas was considered a clever chemist, and it was rumoured that during his final hours in prison he negotiated the sale of a formula for £5000 to provide an income for his daughters after his untimely death.

Mutiny and murder

The British merchant ship *Flowery Land*, with its crew of mixed nationalities, left London in July 1863 bound for Singapore, carrying a cargo of wine, beer, and other goods.

Occasionally, some member of the crew showed insubordination which resulted in punishment, the Mate once or twice using a rope's end on some of the men, and a Greek seaman, George Carlos, was ordered on deck and strapped to the bulwark for a while for refusing to attend to his duty. The captain, however, who seemed a humane man, soon had him released. Although some of the seamen also complained about the food and water, and resented the strict discipline on board, there seemed nothing at that time to hint at an organised mutiny, much less that murder was in the offing.

But some of the crew, six Spaniards, a Turk and a Greek, sprang into action during the afternoon of 10 September. The trouble started during First Mate John Carswell's watch on deck, whilst Captain John Smith was below in his berth. The Captain's brother

EXECUTION of the FIVE PIRATES of the "FLOWERY LAND" SHIP,
on Monday, February 22nd, 1864.
FROM A
PHOTOGRAPH taken on the MORNING of the EXECUTION.
London—Published by Ransom, Bouverie Street.

The execution of the 'Flowery Land' mutineers.

George, and Second Mate William Taffir, were also below. They slept
in the cabin, and some of the crew in quarters on the deck. Carswell
was taken by surprise and was unable to resist as he was struck down
by men using hand spikes. His assailants continually hit him about
the head and face until every feature was obliterated, and still
shrieking for pity, he was tossed into the sea.

Alarmed by the noise, the Captain arose and got as far as the companionway, where he was stabbed to death by 22-year-old Spaniard
Miguel Lopez and the Turk Marcus Vartor (alias Watto), aged 23.
The Captain's brother tried to escape by the companionway ladder,
but he too was attacked and beaten about the head until he died, and

137

his body was thrown into the sea.

The killers then put a rope around the Captain's body, intending to throw it overboard, but Taffir asked to be allowed to sew up the corpse in canvas. This was agreed, and after the last offices had been performed the body was dumped in the water.

Another Spaniard, known only as Marsolino, aged 32, struck the ship's Norwegian carpenter Michael Anderson on the neck with a hand spike, but the victim fortunately survived. Although Spaniard John Lyons (Leone) also 22, was the ringleader and spokesman for the murderous mutineers, it was his fellow countryman Ambrosio Duranno who insisted on taking the dubious credit for killing Carswell. And it was the Greek, George Carlos, who later ordered that they set course for Buenos Aires, so that they might avoid punishment for their crimes. Second Mate William Taffir's life was to be spared, for he was the only man left aboard who understood navigation. He was ordered to take the ship to the River Plate, and when the vessel finally arrived off the coast of South America in early October, it was deliberately scuttled, the criminals and some of the crew leaving in two boats with as much of the cargo as they could take with them.

But the cook, steward and boy lamp trimmer, all Chinese, were abandoned to go down with the sinking ship. The cook was last seen clinging to the wreckage, imploring for mercy, until the waves closed over him.

Taffir revealed later: 'We landed at 4 pm on 4 October, 1863. When we landed Lopez said I was to say the vessel was an American ship from Peru, laden with guano for Bordeaux; that she foundered 100 miles out at sea, and that we had been in the boat for five days and nights. I was also to say that the Captain and others got into a boat in a heavy breeze, but which way they went, or what had become of them, we did not know.'

But the next day, Taffir, accompanied by a French seaman named Candereau, managed to escape unnoticed, and they notified the authorities of the real situation.

The mutineers were eventually captured and returned to England for trial, and because the court found they had conspired together they were considered equally guilty of the murders. Five of the pirates, John Lyons, Francisco Blanco, Ambrosio Duranno, Marcus Watto and Miguel Lopez, were executed outside Newgate Prison on

23 February, 1864. But Basilio de Los Santos and Marsolino were reprieved, and although George Carlos was acquitted of murder, he was later punished for scuttling the ship.

The hangings understandably attracted a record crowd of onlookers, and huge prices were paid for places at windows and on roofs affording a clear view of the old gallows. The authorities, recalling that thirty spectators had been crushed to death in the crowd 57 years earlier at a triple execution, erected suitable barricades and hoardings, as well as providing emergency exits.

Unaccustomed as they were to the rituals associated with Old Bailey hangings, the bemused pirates reacted to their end in differing ways. Blanco, reputedly the most vicious of the bunch, proved cowardly in the extreme, and despite being fortified with brandy he fainted and had to be hanged whilst seated in a chair. Watto was reported resigned to his fate, whilst both Lopez and Lyons showed no signs of fear. Duranno, who was by far the largest and strongest of the men, expressed a great terror of death.

But 63-year-old hangman William Calcraft took it all in his stride, and soon had the murderers dying side by side on his creaking old gibbet.

The First Railway Murder

To Franz Muller, a 24-year-old German tailor, goes the dubious distinction of committing Britain's first railway murder on a warm July night in 1864, and the overwhelming evidence produced at his London trial proved his certain guilt. It was quickly confirmed that he was the villain who had attacked and robbed a Mr Thomas Briggs in a carriage on the North London railway between Bow and Hackney Wick stations. He had then callously thrown his victim's still breathing but insensible body from the train on to the railroad track. When he was arrested some weeks later aboard a ship in Staten Island Bay, America, he was in possession of the dead man's watch and hat.

Muller, who denied the crime, appeared indifferent throughout his trial. On the evening before his execution at Newgate, he was visited by Sheriff Dakin, who noticed that the condemned man was reading a bible. Dakin told him that the promises of forgiveness in the good book rested on the sinner's repentance and confession. After Dakin had left, Muller told a prison officer 'Man has no power to forgive sins, and there is no use in confessing to him.' However, Dr Louis Capell, minister at the German Lutheran Chapel in Alie Street, Whitechapel, who attended the convict at his execution, was determined to save Muller's soul. Only seconds before the killer's death, the pair had the following conversation in their native language.

Capell: 'In a few moments, Muller, you will stand before God; I ask you again, and for the last time, are you guilty or innocent?'

Muller: 'I am innocent.'

Capell: 'You are innocent?'

Muller: 'God Almighty knows what I have done.'

Capell: 'God Almighty knows what you have done? Does God know that you have done this particular deed?'

Muller: 'Yes; I did it.'

A reporter for *The Times* recorded the minister's reaction at this timely admission of guilt. 'So relieved was Dr Cappell by the confession,' he wrote, 'that he rushed from the scaffold exclaiming, "Thank God! Thank God!" and sank down in a chair, completely exhausted by his own emotion.'

Great efforts were made by London's German community to obtain a reprieve for Muller, and even the King of Prussia telegraphed Queen Victoria asking her to spare the murderer's life.

As with others hung since the early 1830s, the body of Muller was buried within the grounds of Newgate. A moving account of what this involved was written at the time of Muller's death:

For those that die upon the scaffold there is not tomb but Newgate ... a tomb such as the few who love the felon best can only live with shuddering hope that it may be forgotten. In Newgate there is no solemnity of burial; it is a mere hurried covering the body of one who was not fit to live among mankind.

So with the corpse of Muller. It had died publicly; the surgeon had certified to its shameful death. Towards the middle of the day the rough deal box which held it was filled with shavings and quick lime, and the warders carried it to the hole where it had to be thrust under the flagstones of a narrow, bleak, gaol pathway.

Muller's body was buried beneath the flagstones of Dead Man's Walk, Newgate.

There, beneath the massive cross-barred gratings which almost shut out the light of day ... there, where none pass the little hidden grave save those who, like himself, must go over it to their own great doom, the body of Muller rests. In a few days the cruelty and singularity of his great crime will be commemorated by a rough 'M' cut in the gaol stone near his head, just as Greenacre, Good and others of the worst are marked beside him.

The Last Man

History records that an anti-British Irish movement, known as the Fenian Society, emerged during the early years of the nineteenth century, and spread to America along with the immigrants who fled Ireland to escape the great famine. In Britain, Fenian terrorist outrages occurred in Chester, Manchester and London, but the organisation officially collapsed in 1867, only quickly to resurface in a new, respectable form under a constitutional mantle. But, alas, its lawlessness never really vanished, and is with us today under the title of the IRA.

A tangible reminder of the Fenian's London activities is still to be seen in the form of a commemorative plaque at the Hugh Myddleton School, Bowling Green Lane, Clerkenwell. It informs the curious that the school occupies the site of the former House of Detention which was built as an overflow to Newgate Prison, and held both men and women awaiting trial during the last century. In fact, the school is yet surrounded by the grim old prison's outer walls, and some of the cells remain intact beneath the building.

The plaque is a reminder that in the winter of 1867 one Michael Barrett, aged 27, led an attempt to free Fenian prisoners from the gaol by blowing up part of the north wall, an act which caused a great loss of life. Barrett was caught and brought to trial, and on 26 May, 1868, he was the last person to be executed in public outside Newgate Prison.

6 Behind closed doors

From the summer of 1868, executions were carried out in the prison yard on a ground-level gallows above a pit, which could comfortably cope with triple hangings. Although members of the press were officially allowed to witness executions, reporters were present solely at the discretion of the prison governor. As the years passed, journalists were progressively discouraged from covering the proceedings. Instead, bland official announcements were made stating that hangings had gone smoothly, with the condemned dying 'instantaneously'.

But the public knew better – mostly due to stories circulated by both prison officers and hangmen in unguarded moments. No doubt the accounts were embellished at each telling, but some real evidence of disturbing mishaps seems to have filtered through the curtain of official silence. In 1875, Mr John Rowland Gibson confirmed that during his forty years as Newgate Prison's surgeon, he had only experienced two executions that had gone perfectly. The remaining victims, he stated publicly, had all slowly strangled to death.

Indeed, executioners were not slow to admit that there was no such thing as a perfect technique of hanging, although some practitioners produced better results than their colleagues. There is no doubt that if an execution was completed without problems, there was an element of luck in the matter. The hangman's dilemma was that if a person was given too long a drop (as occasionally happened well into the present century) then the head could be wholly or partially removed by the fall; but if an insufficient drop was allowed, then this resulted in a slow and painful death by strangulation.

A Bloody Crime

The first person to be executed in private within the walls of Newgate was 18-year-old waiter Alexander Arthur Mackay. He was hanged on 8 September, 1868, after admitting the brutal killing of his employer's wife, Mrs Grossmith, the previous summer.

The noisy crime attracted the attention of neighbours, who spotted Mackay fleeing the scene with blood on his face. They found his still-living victim lying on her back behind a door almost floating in blood. Amazingly, despite her appalling head injuries inflicted with an iron bar and a rolling pin, Mrs Grossmith survived for almost a week before dying. When Mr Grossmith arrived on the scene he could not even recognize his wife because of her disfigurement, and he was horrified at the sight of the blood, some of which had spurted more than eight feet up the walls.

The killer disappeared without trace for over a year, until he was recognized by a sharp-eyed warder at Maidstone Prison where Mackay was being held for a minor crime. On being challenged, the culprit admitted his identity and confessed to the murder.

A reporter who covered the execution for *The Times*, observed: 'Nothing could be more striking than the aspect of Newgate yesterday as contrasted with what it used to be when executions were public. There was no uproar, there were no barriers, and, above all, there was no wolfish crowd of thieves and prostitutes waiting to see a man die ... Death by hanging now means a silent, terrible execution, where the half-dozen or dozen spectators have the painful duty of staying by until the man is hanged until he is dead.'

Of Mackay's end, he commented: 'The sufferings of the murderer were dreadful, but on this we will not dwell, except insofar as to say that in the opinion of those present the fall given was not sufficient to secure instantaneous death.' It is not at all surprising that Mackay had a lingering and agonizing death, for his hanging was performed by the elderly William Calcraft (born 1800), who was notorious for giving his victims a short drop, so that they mostly died from strangulation.

A Victorian Villain

The dangers of leading a double life were exemplified by the fate of Victorian entrepreneur Henry Wainwright, who was hanged at Newgate shortly before Christmas in 1875.

Wainwright, who owned a brushmaking business in East London's Whitechapel Road, was a respected member of local society. He had been apparently happily married for more than a decade, was a devoted churchgoer, and he even lectured on literature and poetry. But in common with so many of his 'respectable' contemporaries, Wainwright was not quite the perfect Victorian gentleman he appeared to be.

Some time prior to his fatal appointment with hangman William Marwood he had acquired a young and attractive mistress, Harriet Lane, whom he kept in a discreet and comfortable lifestyle. But despite his running a successful inherited commercial venture, he found the lady's increasing financial demands troublesome, especially as she soon became the mother of his two children. So he decided that desperate measures were necessary, and he chose the unsophisticated but permanent solution of murder! He shot the unlucky young woman twice in the head, and also cut her throat to ensure that she was dead. After dismembering poor Harriet's corpse, he buried the pieces beneath his workshop floor.

But fate rapidly began to catch up with the callous killer. A search was soon under way for the missing mother, and to add to his problems, Wainwright was declared bankrupt, which meant that he would have to vacate his premises. Meanwhile, the married couple who occupied rooms above his workshop, complained about the awful smell emanating from below. Realising that he had very little time to remove the rotting pieces of his victim's body, Wainwright set about his gruesome task immediately, and had soon packed the parts into manageable parcels. But he slipped up when he left the packages in the care of a youth while he popped out to call a cab. During his absence the young man became curious, and on investigating one particular item was horrified to find that it held a severed human hand.

Wainwright duly made his appearance in the Newgate Prison yard. Minutes before he died, he reportedly sneered at the assembled crowd of some 60 witnesses 'Come to see a man die, have you, you curs?'

A Journey of Horror

Mention the name of Mrs Pearcey to criminologists, and it will immediately conjure up the senseless double murder committed by Mary Eleanor Wheeler in October 1890. Indeed, the brutal killings of Mrs Phoebe Hogg and her infant child may be compared in savagery with any of the Jack the Ripper slayings. But the Kentish

Town murders, as the affair became known, were not only vicious and bloody crimes, they also featured a horrific sequel that shocked the sensibilities of Victorian citizens during that winter long ago.

Wheeler, 24, who preferred to be known as Mrs Pearcey, was the mistress of Frank Samuel Hogg, a furniture-removal man of Prince of Wales Road, Camden Town, who was married, with a wife and a six-month-old daughter, both called Phoebe. Hogg had a key to Wheeler's home in Priory Street, Kentish Town, London, where he used to visit her. Eventually, he introduced Wheeler to his wife, and they all spent a Christmas holiday together. Wheeler fostered the friendship, and she later successfully nursed her lover's 31-year-old wife through a serious illness. Mrs Hogg, then, may not have been too surprised to receive an urgent request to visit Wheeler at her home on the afternoon of 24 October. She obviously responded, for witnesses saw the visitor's pram standing outside the Wheeler's house that day.

Late that Friday evening, Phoebe Hogg's battered body, partly covered with a cardigan, was found dumped on the pavement near a building site in Crossfield Road, Hampstead. The smothered corpse of her baby was discovered on waste ground in the Finchley Road, the following Sunday morning. The blood-stained pram, soon identified as belonging to the dead woman, was found in Hamilton, Terrace, St John's Wood.

Police inquiries produced witnesses who had seen Wheeler pushing a heavy-laden pram (it had held the bodies of the two victims) between Kentish Town and Hampstead, and the large pram must have proved heavy indeed for Wheeler to push through the streets during that long evening three-mile journey of horror. An undertaker said that Mrs Hogg was five feet, six-and-a-half inches tall, and weighed 118 pounds, and the baby weighed 18 pounds.

A post mortem showed that Mrs Hogg had died from fractures to her skull. Her throat had also been cut, and her head was almost severed from her body. A search of Wheeler's home revealed that the kitchen ceiling and windows were splashed with blood. A blood-stained poker and knives were also found, as well as the charred remains of a bonnet on the hearth, and other incriminating items. Wheeler had several scratches on her hands which she claimed were due to her efforts at catching mice which infested her kitchen. She was arrested and charged with murder. But her lover Hogg produced

This is the pram in which Mrs Pearcey somehow managed to wheel her victims' blood-covered bodies to Hampstead.

a perfect alibi which proved that he had taken no part in the cruel killings.

At her trial Wheeler denied the murder charge, but the prosecution alleged that her passion for Hogg had driven her to murder, and that judging from the wounds, the crime must have been committed with merciless savagery. Despite the overwhelming circumstantial evidence against his client, defence counsel Mr Arthur Hutton, said that she was 'a young woman of affectionate and kindly disposition who could not have committed so atrocious a crime.' But the jury disagreed and quickly found her guilty.

After the trial and execution, Hutton revealed a gentler side of his client to the writer Hargrave Lee Adam. He told him: Although undoubtedly guilty of this very brutal murder, she had a most humane side to her character, which was proved, I should think, by her behaviour while in prison. Or, at all events, by one incident alone which occurred during her detention. Birds would daily settle on the sill of her cell window, and she regularly fed them with bread crumbs. It seems almost incongruous, does it not? But there, who is to solve the mysteries of the human heart and mind?'

Shortly before her execution, Wheeler asked her solicitor, Mr F. Freke Palmer, to do her a final favour, and on her behalf he inserted the following mysterious message in a Madrid newspaper: 'M.E.C.P. – Last wish of M.E.W. Have not betrayed.' The message is thought to refer to the killer's secret marriage to an unknown man. But whatever the truth of the matter, it was a secret that Wheeler took with her to the grave.

Although members of the press were not allowed to witness the execution carried out by James Berry on a freezing cold and foggy morning, Wheeler was said to have faced her end in a calm manner, and that her death was instantaneous. On her way to the gallows she reportedly told the chaplain: 'The sentence is just, but the evidence was false.'

A Busy Year for Murder

Executioner James Billington and his assistant William Warbrick carried out the final triple hanging at Newgate Prison on 9 June 1896; and the pair remained overnight to hang baby-farmer Amelia Elizabeth Dyer on the same gallows the following day. The trio of Londoners who met their end together were 46-year-old William Seaman, and partners-in-crime Albert Milsom, 33, and Henry Fowler, 31.

Despite its tragic aspect, there was a distinct element of farce about the discovery, pursuit and capture of double-killer William Seaman, on a bright spring London morning that year. The 'cops and robbers' chase began when he was spotted peeping from a window at the Whitechapel home of retired 74-year-old Jewish businessman Mr John Goodman Levy. An observant neighbour, Mr William Schafer, knowing that the corner house was usually only occupied by Mr Levy and his resident housekeeper, sent for the police after seeing the strange intruder. The policemen, who entered the house by an unlocked back door, were shocked to find the bodies of the old man and his housekeeper, Mrs Sarah Annie Gale, with their throats cut. Mr Levy's bloody corpse was discovered huddled in a downstairs closet, and the woman's in a bedroom. The house had been ransacked.

By this time a crowd of curious spectators, attracted by the police activity, had gathered around the house, and a policeman, on looking up, saw a man trying to hide behind a parapet. The officer ran indoors and up into the top floor front room, where he found a hole had been cut in the ceiling. Climbing through the hole, he made his way on to the roof, where he saw Seaman some fifteen yards away. The policeman called out, panicking Seaman, who then jumped some forty feet down into the street below, landing in the middle of the throng. The badly injured and unconscious criminal was carried into the back parlour of the house by policemen, while other officers retrieved jewellery and cash which had fallen from his pockets.

It was claimed that Seaman later admitted the murders, saying that he killed Mr Levy in revenge because the man had once swindled him.

Milsom and Fowler were executed for the murder of elderly Henry Smith, whilst burgling his home at Muswell Hill in February. The victim was beaten to death defending his property, before the killers stole £112 cash from his safe. The villains fled to Wales, where they joined up with a travelling sideshow for which they provided financial backing. But intensive police investigations led officers to Bath in April, where they surprised and arrested the murderers. The pair blamed each other for the brutal killing, and during their Old Bailey trial Fowler tried to attack Milsom in the dock, but the scuffle was broken up by police and prison officers.

The duo kept their date with destiny on Newgate's gallows, with William Seaman placed between them, at the triple hanging. Even then, the drama was not quite ended, for whilst assistant executioner Warbrick was strapping one of the murderer's legs, hangman James Billington prematurely pushed the lever and Warbrick fell through the open trap door. He nevertheless miraculously managed to avoid injury by clinging to one of the killer's legs as he dropped.

The infamous deeds of baby-farmer Mrs Amelia Elizabeth Dyer shocked the nation in that same year of 1896. In March, a bargeman hooked a brown paper parcel from the River Thames at Caversham Lock beside Reading railway station, and was horrified to find that it contained the corpse of a 15-month-old child. The toddler, which had been strangled with a piece of tape which was still around its throat, was wrapped in napkins of paper, and weighed down with a brick. Amazingly, police found that a piece of the wrapping paper bore a name and address: Mrs Harding, 20 Wiggott's Road, Caversham. Although the address was false, police eventually traced a house at Piggott's Road, which in turn led them to Dyer at her home in Kensington Road, Reading. There they learned that the small, fat 57-year-old nurse was in the habit of frequently changing both her name and address. The house was also filled with baby clothes. However, before the police had knocked on Dyer's door, two more toddlers were discovered in a carpet bag which had been dumped in the river near Caversham Weir Head, and four other unidentified babies' bodies were recovered from the water nearby.

The first dead child was later identified as Helena Fry, the illegitimate offspring of a Bristol servant girl who had paid Dyer £15 to take the infant off her hands, after assurance that it would have 'a happy home and a mothers' loving care'. Those in the bag were named as Doris Marmon and Harry Simmons. Doris was also illegitimate, the daughter of Cheltenham barmaid Evelina Edith Marmon. The mother had handed over her child, and a £10 fee, after answering Dyer's advertisement in the *Bristol Times and Mirror*. Harry was likewise of dubious parentage, his mother a lady's maid who had abandoned the boy at the Dyer household, to be promptly murdered.

When arrested, Dyer, a widow who had a Salvation Army background, was said to have appeared prematurely old. Her only defence was that she was insane and not responsible for her actions, but the evidence against her proved conclusive. Dr L. Forbes Winslow, an eminent Victorian psychiatrist, appeared on her behalf. He said she had made several suicide attempts in earlier years, and that in his opinion she suffered from 'delusional insanity'. He added that she was a former mental patient, and 'saw visions and heard voices'. But the outraged jurors rejected Dyer's insanity plea and convicted her of wilful murder. She was hanged at Newgate on 10 June.

Some years after her execution, four babies' skeletons were unearthed in the garden of a Bristol house where Dyer had once lived, and it transpired that Dyer had operated as a baby-farmer for some 15 years. The number of her victims will never be known.

Two years after Dyer's death, her daughter Mrs Polly Palmer and son-in-law Arthur Ernest Palmer were convicted of abandoning a three-week-old baby girl in a railway carriage at Newton Abbot. They had accepted the baby for adoption and a fee of £14. They had then undressed the child, wrapped it in brown paper and dumped it

Madame Tussaud's waxwork of Mrs Dyer, who murdered the babies for whom she promised to find good homes.

beneath a carriage seat, where it was not found until the following day. The heartless couple were each sentenced to two years' hard labour – it seems that they were continuing the family tradition!

End of an Era

French anarchist Martial Faugeron made his mark in British criminal history by being the last person to be executed at Newgate Prison, in November 1901. The 23-year-old was hanged by James Billington after murdering Clerkenwell watchmaker Mr Hermann Francis Jung. The killer had turned to crime to raise cash to support his revolutionary aspirations, but he was quickly caught and punished.

Faugeron's violent death ended an era of judicial slayings at Newgate, and the subsequent demolition of the ancient gaol saw the demise of centuries of prison misery. But the sinister site of untold sufferings nevertheless continues its association with crime, death and punishment. For the prison was replaced with London's Central Criminal Courts building – the Old Bailey – where still is heard an endless catalogue of horrific deeds.

7 Relics of Crime

Whilst preparing the present book, I determined to discover what relics of the terrible old gaol and its contemporary London counterparts are still to be found in the city.

By its very nature, the Chamber of Horrors at the famous Madame Tussaud's waxworks exhibition, at London's Baker Street, is replete with exhibits culled from the fearful old prison. On display there is a door from the condemned cell, a lock and keys, the door bell and the larger prison bell which was tolled to announce executions, and some contemporary literature. Items in store include the contents of the former home of Kentish Town murderess Eleanor Wheeler, alias Mrs Pearcey. The goods were bought for £200 for exhibition, and the cash went towards the killer's defence costs. After Wheeler's execution, a tableau went on show featuring the dead woman's sittingroom and bedroom, complete with her possessions. A wax model of Wheeler was included, depicting her leaning against a mantelpiece. But the 30,000 morbid visitors attracted to the Chamber of Horrors in that winter of 1890 no doubt wanted to see the other, more gruesome, items on display. These included the bloodstained clothing removed from the murdered bodies, a piece of the dead baby's toffee, wax masks of the pitiful victims, and the pram which had held their corpses.

Colonel Edward Marcus Despard, who was hanged and beheaded at Horsemonger Lane Gaol after unsuccessfully plotting the assassination of King George III in 1803, also has a further claim to dubious fame! His was the first English character that Madame Tussaud figured in wax following her arrival in Britain in 1802. Alas, the effigy has long since disappeared, but the notorious Colonel is commemorated in a surviving waxworks poster dated c. 1804. Also lost to posterity is the death mask of Benjamin Courvoisier, the 23-year-old servant who savagely slaughtered his master, Lord William

Russell, in 1840, but a photograph of the item remains on file. Other memorabilia kept by Tussaud's includes a cheque signed by ladykiller Henry Wainwright, and relics of Frederick and Maria Manning, who murdered Maria's lover – there still exists a model of the kitchen in which the crime was committed, a contemporary broadsheet, and most interesting of all, Frederick's handwritten letter of confession.

The Museum of London also has its share of grim exhibits associated with Newgate. One of them provides a forbidding reminder of a darker age in London's history. This is the former prison's reconstructed Debtors' Door and Lodge through which so many people passed to their doom. There is also a cell with its original wooden-lined walls bearing period graffiti in the form of carved inscriptions, initials, names and dates. Another item which attracts the visitors' awed attention is the gaol's old whipping post. This was much used by executioner William Calcraft, for his duties included flogging young offenders. Also displayed are some Newgate prison keys, convicts' tokens and a small crucifix carved out of mutton bone, as well as illustrations depicting various aspects of The Cato Street Conspiracy. There is also a collection of objects relating to the 'watch' (policing) system, including warning rattles, swords, truncheons and documents.

Other mementos including dining plates once used by Newgate inmates and a charred prison beam which survived the Gordon Riots are carefully kept at St Sepulchre's Church in Newgate Street, opposite the Old Bailey. The nearby 'Viaduct Tavern', a splendid Victorian hostelry, boasts cellars which were once part of the old gaol.

A more general London prison theme exists south of the River Thames, in a permanent crime and punishment exhibition held in the surviving ancient Clink debtors' prison at St Saviour's Dock, located on the historic Bankside waterfront, in an area redolent of timeless misery. The word Clink worked its way into the English language to become synonymous for prison, and the sign of the fiddle hanging outside the prison gates obviously implied 'being on the fiddle'.

The convict theme is also perpetuated at the adjacent seventeenth century pub, 'The Anchor', once a favourite watering hole of writers Dr Samuel Johnson, Oliver Goldsmith and James Boswell, actor David Garrick, artist Sir Joshua Reynolds and Irish Statesman Edmund Burke. The historic tavern is decorated with thumbscrews,

The doors to the condemned cell, Newgate.

convicts' irons and an assortment of genuine and gruesome well-used leather execution pinion straps.

These are just a selection of the prison paraphernalia still extant in London. Many more remain tucked away in private collections, dusty storerooms, attics and antiques shops, awaiting the time when they will be identified and restored to the public gaze.

Appendix: Some Sources for Genealogists

After initially confirming through the British Library's catalogue of printed books that Mr Baker's diary had not been published, I set out to corroborate the record of people and events he had described. Knowing that Newgate Prison was the Common Gaol for the City of London and the County of Middlesex, I consulted the sessions papers (verbatim court reports) held at London's Guildhall Library in book form, and some contemporary publications.

Period newspapers can be a very rich source of information, and many of these are deposited at The British Library Newspaper Library, Colindale Avenue, London NW9 5HE, which has a comprehensive catalogue (enquiry desk telephones: 071-636 1544 and 071-323 7353/5/6).

I also visited London's Lambeth Palace Library, by appointment, in a vain attempt to trace Baker as a clergyman. Sources consulted there were: *Novum Repertorium* (London diocesan clergy succession from the earliest times to 1898) by George Hennessy (H5107.L8); and *Alumni Cantabrigienses* by J. A. Venn, Part II 1752–1900; Abbey Challis.

A useful way of tracking down some Middlesex and London names is to consult the *Middlesex Calendar of Indictments*, held at 40 Northampton Road, London E.C.1. Indictments are, in fact, criminal charge sheets, and they follow a standard pattern, giving the name of the accused, domicile, status or occupation, and details of the offence, with a note of the sentence added later. But information on the indictments must be treated with a certain amount of caution, as they can be misleading. The listed domicile is usually the parish where the crime was committed, and therefore not necessarily the prisoner's place of residence or origin. Likewise, the status or occupation is usually expressed in general terms such as 'labourer' or 'single woman'. It must be emphasized that no other personal information is given in indictments, although on the reverse sides of some of these documents are lists of witnesses.

For those seeking details of sailors, then a search of the Admiralty Records kept at the Public Record Office, Chancery Lane, London WC2A 1LR is essential. The National Maritime Museum at Greenwich, as well as the Public Record Office, Kew, are also well worth consulting.

The case of the former policeman, William Hill, mentioned in Baker's diary, prompted research into the policing situation in the nineteenth century. The Worship Street establishment, where Hill once served, was one of seven police offices set up in 1792. They each had six constables (by 1822 this had been increased to eight), three Justices of the Peace, clerks and ancillary staff, and they operated around London. They were similar to Bow Street, and their police-men investigated crimes and brought criminals to the magistrates for trial. The possibilities for collusion between police officers and criminals were tempting – Hill was discharged for taking a bribe and allowing a prisoner to escape. There are many other examples in the records of officers and villains making mutually profitable deals with the owners of property for its return – the owners, in fact, paid for police investigations.

There is a series of Parliamentary Papers on policing, and on prisons, for the early part of the nineteenth century. They comprise the *Reports of the Select Committees of the House of Commons*, which inves-tigated by interviewing witnesses (the testimony is included) and collecting statistics before making their reports. Police and prisons were taken together because the arguments were all about expendi-ture, which the House was supervising. Occasionally, they visited the prisons or convict ships.

Here follows a rather daunting list of reports, which may at first appear somewhat obscure, but much of the eyewitness testimonies is rivetting stuff, providing as it does a final word on social conditions in Regency times:

1810: 25th Report from the Select Committee on Finance (1798 reprinted 1810): Police, including convict establishments.
1812: Select Committee on the Nightly Watch and Policing of the Metropolis.
1816: Reports from the Select Committee on the State of the Police of the Metropolis.

1817: First Report from the Select Committee on the State of the Police of the Metropolis.
1817: Second Report from the Select Committee on the State of the Police of the Metropolis.
1818: Third Report from the Select Committee on the State of the Police of the Metropolis.
1822: Report from the Select Committee on the Policing of the Metropolis.
1828: Report from the Select Committee on the Policing of the Metropolis.

In the Introduction to the 1822 Report, the Committee says it considered in 1816, 1817 and 1818: the system of licensing public houses, the establishment of penitentiary prisons, the extent and effect of female prostitution, the conditions in Tothill, Clerkenwell and Cold Bath Prisons, the state and expenditure of the different police establishments in the Metropolis.

All this material is held at the British Library, but researchers may find many of these Parliamentary Papers more easily accessible at the University of London Library's reference section at Senate House, Malet Street, London, where day tickets are available at the 4th floor membership desk for bona fide researchers. Some other London libraries also keep copies of these fascinating reports.

Staff at the Archives Authority of New South Wales, 2 Globe Street, The Rocks, Sydney 2000, Australia, also kindly provided me with badly-needed information through the mail.

Readers who are interested in convict transportation (deportation) may wish to consult documents held by the Public Record Office, Ruskin Avenue, Kew, Richmond, Surrey TW9 4DU, in England. Some of the suggested sources there are:

Ref: HO 7(2) – Convicts, Miscellaneous (1785–1835) Minutes of House of Commons Committee regarding transportation to West Africa 1785, and correspondence and papers of the Home Office and the convict establishment, 1823 to 1835, including returns of deaths of convicts in New South Wales, and reports on conditions of convict prisons and hulks in the United Kingdom and the Colonies.

Ref: HO 8(1) – Convict Prisons (1824–1876) Sworn lists of convicts on board the hulks (ship prisons) and in convict prisons with details of ages, convictions, sentences, health, behaviour, etc.

Ref: HO 11(5) – Convict Transportation Registers, 1787–1870 Lists of convicts transported in various ships, giving the details of their convictions.

State Papers Third Report for the Committee on the laws relating to Penitentiary Houses, 1812; Select Committee on Transporta-tion, 1837; Report from the Select Committee on Transportation, 1837.

Manuscript Material (Overseas) Convict Records, Governors' Minutes and Colonial Secretary In and Out Letters – Archives Authority of New South Wales, Sydney, Australia; Convict Records – Archives Office of Tasmania, Hobart.

Acknowledgements

The author and publishers would like to thank all those who have helped with illustrations for this book. We endeavoured to trace copyright wherever necessary, and apologise if there are acknow-ledgements thereby omitted. p.21: Greater London Record Office; p. 141: Guildhall Library, London; pp. 133, 148, 151, 155: Madame Tussaud's; pp. 14, 137: Donald Rumbelow; p. 124: Tower Hamlets Local History Library, London.